KHAJURAHO

Acknowledgements

I have been doing research in Khajuraho for the past five years and have written four books on Khajuraho. Each time I write I am reminded of the number of people to whom I am indebted.

I would like to thank:

The Guidebook Company, Hong Kong, particularly Geoff Cloke and Magnus Bartlett who have encouraged and guided me along the way;

Kamal Sahai for his companionship and for enriching this book with his photographs;

everyone in Gulmohur Press for their support in this project, especially Ajay Verma for assisting in design and layout;

the Archaeological Survey of India for permission to photograph the historical monuments under their care - taking this opportunity of expressing my humble appreciation for the immense efforts they have put into maintaining and preserving the temples of Khajuraho;

everyone in Khajuraho for helping me over the years;

a special note of thanks to all my friends who have made Khajuraho the special place it is.

KHAJURAHO
AND ITS
HISTORIC SURROUNDINGS

Shobita Punja
Photography by Kamal Sahai

Dr Shobita Punja was born in South India and studied in various schools in India, Beirut and London. She has a Bachelor's Degree in Art History, a Master's Degree in Ancient Indian History, another Master's Degree in Art Education from Stanford University, California. Shobita's doctoral research was also in the field of Art Education, and subsequently she spent fifteen years working with the Ministry of Education and Culture. Her recent study has been in the interpretation of the temples of Khajuraho. **Divine Ecstacy, The Story of Khajuraho**, an innovative study was published by Viking in 1992. Other books by her include **Museums of India, Khajuraho** and **Benaras** in Our World in Colour series. Her most recent book, **Great Monuments of India, Bhutan, Nepal, Pakistan, and Sri Lanka** was published by the Guidebook Company, Hong Kong, in 1994.

Kamal Sahai began his career as a journalist. He soon took to photography and has contributed to several newspapers, magazines and books. He carried out the first complete photographic documentation of the Crafts of Jammu, Kashmir and Ladakh, which was published by Mapin. He has recently published his photographs of Calcutta in The Guidebook Company series Our World in Colour.

First published in 1994 by The Guidebook Company Limited, Hong Kong
Ground Floor, 15 Lower Kai Yuen Lane, North Point, Hong Kong

ISBN: 962-217-395-0

Photographs by Kamal Sahai

Maps by Ripin Kalra

Designed by Gulmohur Press, New Delhi.
Produced by Twin Age Limited, Hong Kong

Printed in Hong Kong

Contents

THE LAND   11
  Climate   12
  Flora   13
  Fauna   14
  Bird Life   15

HISTORY   18
  The Chandella Rulers   19
  Khajuraho Rediscovered 21
  Religion   24
  The Temple   26

THE STORY OF KHAJURAHO   28

WHAT TO SEE IN KHAJURAHO   33
  Shiv Sagar tank   36
  Chausat Yogini Temple   36
  Matangeshvar Temple   37

WESTERN GROUP OF TEMPLES   40
  Devi Mandap   40
  Varaha Mandap   40
  Lakshman Temple   41
  Kandariya Mahadev Temple 45
  Mahadev Shrine   48
  Devi Jagadambi Temple   50
  Chitragupta Temple   51
  Nandi Mandap   52
  Vishvanath Temple   53

EASTERN GROUP OF TEMPLES   62
  Khajuraho Village   62
  Brahma Temple   63
  Javari Temple   63
  Vamana Temple   65

JAIN GROUP OF TEMPLES   68
  Parshvanath Temple   68
  Adhinath Temple   69

SOUTHEASTERN GROUP
OF TEMPLES   72
  Duladeo Temple   72
  Chaturbhuj Temple   73

ARCHAEOLOGICAL
SITE MUSEUM   74

BEYOND KHAJURAHO   80
  Jhansi   80
  Datia   80
  Orccha   82
  Jarai Math Temple   86
  Dhubela Museum   86
  Raneh Waterfalls   86
  Mahoba   87
  Benisagar Lake   87
  Ranguan Lake   87
  Gangau Dam   87
  Rajgarh Palace   88
  Ken River   89
  Panna National Park   90
  Pandav Falls   90
  Panna   90
  Panna Diamond Mines   91
  Ajaygarh   91
  Kalanjar   94
  Nacchna   94
  Bandhavgarh
    National Park 95

HOW TO PLAN YOUR VISIT   97

FACTS FOR THE TRAVELLER   99
  International Travel   99
  Visas   99
  Time Zones   99
  Internal Travel   99
  Security   101
  Currency   101
  Electricity   101
  Health   101
  Hotel Bills   103
  Tipping   104
  Languages   104
  Media   104
  Numbers and
    Measurements   104
  Communications   105
  Photography   105
  Working Hours and
    Holidays   106

INFORMATION ABOUT
  KHAJURAHO   108
  Location   108
  Climate   108
  When to go   109
  What to wear   109
  How to get there   109
  Distances to Khajuraho   111
  People   112
  Where to Stay   112
    Luxury Hotels   112
    Medium-priced Hotels   114
    Budget Hotels   116
  Important Khajuraho
    Telephone Numbers   118

Where to Eat   119
Drinking   120
Banks and Money Changers   121
Post and Telegraph Offices   121
Tourist Information Counters   122
Hospital   123
Entrance to the Temple
  Complex and Museum   123
Photography   123
Shopping   123
Special Festivals at
  Khajuraho   124
Guides   126
Excursion Agents   126
How to get around   127

GLOSSARY   129

FURTHER READING   140

INDEX   142

EXCERPTS
  Captain T.S. Burt *on discovery
    of Khajuraho, 1839*   22-23
  Louis Rousselet *on a festival
    at Khajuraho, 1875*   58-59

MAPS AND PLANS
  Plan of Khajuraho   12
  Devi Jagadambi Temple   27
  Western Group of Temples   33
  Lakshman Temple   41
  Eastern Group of Temples   62
  Madhya Pradesh   76
  Beyond Khajuraho   77

THE LAND

The beautiful little village of Khajuraho lies in the central state of Madhya Pradesh in Chattarpur district. Madhya Pradesh is the largest Indian state covering a land area of over 443,000 square kilometres. The Vindhyan range runs through Madhya Pradesh. The hills are not as high but far older than the Himalayan mountains. The rock bed of Chattarpur district is of fine Bundelkhand gneiss, and is believed to be the oldest rock in India. It is streaked with crystalline quartz, which over the millennia have created steep jagged hillocks that pierce the otherwise flat landscape of Chattarpur district. The most dramatic natural formation to be seen within the visual limits of Khajuraho are the **Dantla hills**. Marking the eastern edge of the village these sharp white peaks emerge above the tree-line like a row of worn-out teeth and are affectionately known as Dantla or the Teeth.

Above the gneiss layer is a bed of sandstone. In the vicinity of Khajuraho the Vindhya hills have produced a very fine sandstone which was used in the construction of the temples. Sandstone being a sedimentary rock is prone to pits and cracks, and much of the sculpture of Khajuraho reveals the damage caused by weathering and the brittleness of the stone. The sandstone is a pale yellow or biscuit colour, its hue altering perceptibly with the play of sunlight and moonlight. The quality of the sandstone also enabled the artists to carve images with minute details that represent the most intricate jewellery, elaborate hairstyles, and the subtle texture of fine textiles.

Nowhere does the state of Madhya Pradesh meet the sea. Yet from the mountains, valleys and ravines of the Vindhyas rise the magnificent and much-revered rivers of the state: the Narmada, Son, Chambal and the Ken or Kiyen, which is closest to Khajuraho. Rivers such as the Betwa (near Orccha), Chambal, Sind, Parbati, Tons and the Ken all follow a northerly direction till they ultimately meet the River Ganga, the holiest of all rivers in India. The Ken is a perennial river, though it is no longer navigable as it has been dammed along its course. Near Khajuraho the Ken has banks of red sandstone, and now and again the river plunges through sandstone gorges creating magical waterfalls and peaceful pools.

(Preceding pages) Mahwa tree, the rural setting of Khajuraho
(Opposite page) Sunset on the Western Group of Temples

Climate

Madhya Pradesh is a geographical region of great variety. The western part of the state is dry, while the central and northern region in which Khajuraho lies is well watered and relatively fertile. To the east are the bamboo forests of Bandhavgarh and further in that direction the great forests of Chattisgarh and Bastar.

Summers in Khajuraho area can be extremely hot, with temperatures rising to 47 degrees Celsius or 117 degrees Fahrenheit. The hot, dry summer of Khajuraho is broken by monsoon showers that arrive in the months of June and July. A moderate monsoon serves to refill the village tanks and feed the surrounding forests. Between winter and spring (November and March) the climate in Khajuraho is pleasant, with temperatures reaching a low of 4 degrees Celsius. This moderate climate and mountainous countryside has created a rich variety of local flora and fauna. It is a lovely time to visit, picnic and wander amidst the temples.

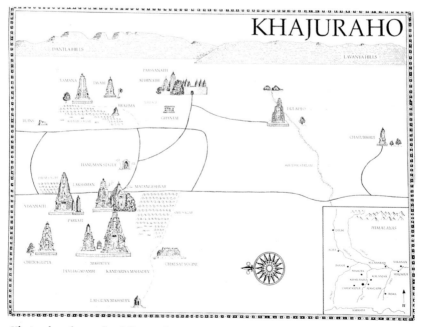

Khajuraho, drawn by Julian Roberts, 1991.

Flora

The deciduous forest nearest to Khajuraho is now protected within the Panna National Park (32 kilometre away). The forest rises from the east bank of the Ken river and covers the plateaux and hillsides. It consists largely of **teak** (*Tectona grandis*), a tree of great beauty and economic value. The tree is tall and elegant with large leaves, some a foot long. When the leaves dry they are reduced to a skeleton of veins that have an interesting appearance when the sunlight passes through them. Just after the monsoons the teak trees are covered with scented pyramids of white blossoms.

The most cherished tree in Khajuraho and its neighborhood is the **mahwa** (*Bassia latifolia*). It grows to a stately height of 15 metres, its spreading branches making it also a pleasant shade tree. The leaves are clustered at the end of branches and are a blazing coppery brown colour when new. The flowers are cream coloured, fleshy and edible. When the flowers drop from the tree they ferment and diffuse a sickly sweet smell into the air. The local people harvest the seed of the *mahwa* for the extraction of oil, the flower and the fruit are eaten as a vegetable or used to prepare a very intoxicating drink. There are long avenues of *mahwa* trees on the Bamitha – Khajuraho road and in the fields and the villages around. A number of old *mahwa* trees grow within the area encompassing the Western Group of Temples.

The **mango** (*Mangifera indica*) tree also grows in the environs of Khajuraho. This is a large, shady evergreen tree which grows to a height of 10 to 15 metres. The trunk is dark and rough, its leaves simple, long and tapering. Between March and May the *mango* tree is covered with clusters of brownish-white flowers that infuse the breeze with a heady fragrance. The fruit of the mango grows from a small green paisley shape to a firm, fully ripe form. The fruit is orange-green outside and inside it is succulent and brilliant orange in colour. To eat a good ripe mango is among the few joys that the burning Indian summer offers, and Khajuraho is surrounded by avenues and orchards of mango trees.

The **neem** (*Azadirachta indica*) is one of the most important and best loved Indian tree. It is a tall tree that grows to over 15 metres and is very shady. The small leaves have a serrated, toothed margin and a single twig is composed of pairs of leaflets. The tree has many medicinal qualities: the twigs are used to clean the teeth and the leaves have a disinfectant effect. A grand old *neem* tree shades Raja Cafe opposite the Western Group of Temples.

The **mulberry tree** (to the right of the Lakshman Temple) has serrated leaves and the sweetest possible fruit appear on it in April.

The lovely **Camel Hoof Trees** (*Bauhinia purpurea*) is locally called *kachnar*. A beautiful line of these trees stand behind the Matangeshvar temple and they burst into bloom between February and March when they are covered with delicate white and pink flowers and not a single leaf.

An indigenous flowering tree of great beauty is the **Flame of the Forest**, locally called *palas* (*Butea monosperma*). It is a short, twisted, gnarled tree which is quite unattractive when devoid of flowers, but in March and April it glows with fleshy fiery orange flowers.

Unfortunately the flowers and flowering shrubs grown in the temple complex are not indigenous to the region. Many flowering trees and shrubs such as the **bougainvillaea** were introduced into India from Europe and England a century ago. The Archaeological Survey of India appears to be partial to this sturdy, vibrantly coloured, plant which requires little water or maintenance and presents a 'pretty picture' to tourists!

Fauna

Khajuraho is extremely fortunate that much of the wild life of the region is protected within the **National Parks of Panna and Bandhavgarh**. Here forms of deer, the Indian gazelle, wild boar and tiger are still to be seen. The sculptured panels of the **Lakshman Temple** in Khajuraho depict scenes of royal hunts for deer and wild boar, with courtiers astride magnificent caparisoned horses. The temple sculptures of Khajuraho also suggest that this region was once the home of the regal Asian elephant. Up to the seventeenth century elephants did inhabit many parts of central India, but with the shrinkage of their habitat they are no longer to be found in the state of Madhya Pradesh.

Within Khajuraho village the hard-working domesticated cattle and buffalo are seen ploughing the fields, threshing grain, or turning the water mill. At night the cattle are brought home and sleep in the courtyard of the hut with their owners' family.

Clambering over the temples and chasing their friends from tree to tree is the grey langur (*Presbytis entelluss*). The langur is pale grey with long limbs and tail, and a dark face. A playful creature who does not usually pester the tourist, he is convinced that the temples of Khajuraho belong to him.

Much quieter and more timid is the lovely five-striped palm squirrel (*Funambulus pennanti*). This little creature is clothed in pale grey fur and has a long tail. Down the head and the back are three dark black and two pale stripes. According to Hindu mythology Ram, the super hero of the epic Ramayana, stroked the squirrel with his fingers and the markings on his back commemorate this divine blessing. The squirrel is seen scuttling over the temples and the trees in a never-ending quest for fruit and seeds to eat.

Bird Life

In and around Khajuraho there is a variety of bird life. For more information *see* Odyssey photographic **Guide to the Birds of India** by Bikram Grewal.

Apart from the common Indian crow, sparrow, myna, pigeon, bulbuls and flocks of parakeets, there are many other lovely birds that you will encounter on your visit to the temples of Khajuraho.

The most beautiful bird that somersaults in the air over the waters and the gardens of Khajuraho is the **Indian Roller** (*Coracias benghalensis*). The bird is pale brown above, and when it opens it wings to fly reveals bright turquoise and dark blue bands on its wings and tail. In Hindu mythology it is named after Shiva, which perhaps accounts for the frequency of the sudden flash of blue encountered all over Khajuraho.

Beside the Shiv Sagar, Prem Sagar and Khajur Sagar reservoirs of Khajuraho there is a thriving population of water fowl.

The **Little Grebe** (*Podiceps ruficollis*) is the smallest Indian water-bird. It is brown, with a shiny rufous neck, and can be seen diving into the water in search of insects and frogs.

The **Large Egret** (*Ardea alba*) is a tall, snow-white marsh bird with a yellow beak. You will see it patiently stalking insects and fish in the shallow waters. There are in addition many herons and cormorants near these waters.

Another astonishing blue bird is the **White-breasted Kingfisher** (*Halcyon smyrnensis*). It sits on telephone wires and high branches overlooking the water waiting to dive and catch a fish or a sizable insect with its long beak. It has a lovely chestnut-brown head and underbody, a white bib over the breast and brilliant turquoise-blue wings.

Near Khajur Sagar live a pair of resident **Sarus Cranes** (*Grus antigone*). They are lovely birds with long legs, grey plumage and red upper neck and head. They spend their time with their long necks bent in constant search of food in the marshes. It is said that the Sarus crane mates for life and the couple embody a perfect symbol of Khajuraho.

The **Hoopoe** (*Upupa epos*) is commonly seen with its long curved beak to the ground on the lawns of the Western Group of Temples at Khajuraho. The bird is a lovely fawn colour with black and brown markings on its wings, back and tail. A black and white-tipped crest surmounts its elegant head.

A pair or several pairs of **Common Grey Hornbills** frequent the trees of the Western Group of Temples. It is a wonderful sight to see these prehistoric-looking birds floating gracefully past the temples in undulating flight. The birds are a pale grey colour with long tails and remarkably elongated, bulbous, curved yellow beaks.

Flitting amidst the flowering trees and shrubs around the temples is the **Black Drongo** (*Dicrurus adsimilis*), a shiny black bird with a long, markedly forked tail.

The Seven Sisters, **Babblers** (*Turdoides caudatus*) are invariably seen in groups around trees and shrubs. Drab brown in colour, they can be heard chattering noisily as they feed and play.

Hovering amidst the flowers, its tiny wings madly aflutter, is the **Purple Sunbird** (*Nectarina asiatica*). The male is a spectacular glossy metallic black - blue (especially dazzling in the sunlight) and the female a yellowish shade. Its curved beak, oversized for its tiny body, is used to draw the nectar from flowers. High above, circling the skies, are kites (*Milvus migrans govinda*) and vultures.

History

History

Madhya Pradesh is a land of great antiquity. In the vicinity of Bhopal, the capital city, there are Stone Age caves with remains of paintings that are 8,000 years old. Madhya Pradesh is the home of monuments representative of various periods of history. Best known amongst them are the great Buddhist monuments of the 2nd century BC and 2nd century AD at Sanchi. In the 3rd - 4th centuries AD the region of Madhya Pradesh came under the administrative control of the Gupta Empire. Excavations at Khajuraho have shown that this area was occupied in the late Gupta period. When Gupta power began to wane in northern and central India, the empire broke up and fell into the hands of regional rulers and feudal lords. The Prathiharas became one of the dominant forces here and ruled between the 6th and 9th centuries. Near Khajuraho the Prathiharas built the Teli-ki-Mandir in Gwalior Fort and the little temple of Jarai Math on the Jhansi - Khajuraho road. Within the village of Khajuraho there is evidence of Prathihara occupation. Small brick and stone structures, and the **Brahma** and the **Lalguan Mahadev** temples in Khajuraho are assigned by historians to this period.

Chandella inscription, Vishvanath Temple

The Chandella Rulers

By the tenth century Prathihara power in the region began to wane. Feudal lords serving under the Prathiharas broke free and established their own independent kingdoms. The rise from obscurity to royal pre-eminence of these tribal chieftains and Rajput clans is shrouded in mystery, and there are few historical accounts to explain how the transformation occurred. It is however clear that one such family came to power in the area of Khajuraho, and in time they came to be known as the Chandellas.

Local legend has it that the founder of the Chandella dynasty was a child born to a young Brahmin woman who had an intimate and brief love affair with the Moon god. The pregnant mother was advised by the gods to go to Khajuraho to give birth to the baby boy who would one day be king and carve out an enormous empire for himself. As the child grew up he proved to be ex-traordinarily brave, killing a wild tiger with his bare hands. Such legends are commonplace in history, concocted by 'upstart' rulers seeking to give divine legitimacy to their authority and kingship.

The history of the rise to power of the Chandella dynasty is recorded in several stone and copperplate inscriptions found in Khajuraho and other areas of the Chandella kingdom. The inscriptions tell us that the dynasty derived its name, Chandella, from the legendary sage, Chandratreya, a descendent of the celebrated sage Atri, in turn descended from the Moon. Rajput clans of north - western and central India are divided into the Surya *vamsha* and the Chandra *vamsha* (sun and moon clans) and claim their respective royal lineage from the sun or the moon.

According to the inscriptions, the first Chandella ruler was Nannuka, credited with establishing the dynasty. He is followed by three rulers, Vakapati, Jayashakti and Vijayashakti who, through a series of battles, expanded the boundaries of their kingdom.

Chandella rulers, patrons of Khajuraho. Archaeological Site Museum

Then came Rahila whose name was given to the little temple, village and tank of Rahilya near Mahoba (55 kilometres from Khajuraho). Rahila's son was Harsha, who is believed to have finally broken away from the Prathihara overlords and established an independent Chandella empire.

Following the brilliant rule of his father Harsha, Yashovarman inherited the Chandella throne. One of his major achievements was the capture and occupation of the magnificent fort of Kalanjar 90 kilometres from Khajuraho. (*See chapter* Beyond Khajuraho). The dominating fort of Kalanjar was one of the main gateways into central India and crucial for its control. Several times in the centuries that followed the sultans and rulers of Delhi laid siege on the fort but the Chandellas succeeded in maintaining their supremacy there till the 13th century. Yashovarman's son and successor was Dhanga. So prestigious an event was the capture of the fort that Dhanga gave himself the honourable title of Shri Kalanjaradhipati, Master of Kalanjar.

One of the royal inscriptions mentions that Yashovarman built a temple to Vishnu and a large tank at Khajuraho. Dhanga, the eighth in line of succession also built a huge temple for Shiva, and within it were installed

two images, one of emerald and one in stone. Dhanga lived to the ripe old age of one hundred years and died in 1002.

The great Chandella ruler Dhanga was succeeded by a line of kings who spent most of their time warding off attacks from the north. During the warring years the Chandellas strengthened their major forts at Kalanjar and Ajaygarh. Paramardideva or Paramardin, the eighteenth Chandella ruler was the last great Chandella monarch. He fought with legendary bravery to save his capital Mahoba and his kingdom from the forces of Prithviraj Chauhan of Delhi. In 1203 Qutub-ud-Din Aibak, the Sultan of Delhi, besieged Kalanjar and killed Paramardin.

Lion, emblem of the Chandellas

Khajuraho Rediscovered

Very few historical records tell us about the fate of Khajuraho between the 13th and 17th centuries. Around 1335, Ibn Batuta, a traveller from north Africa describes a place called Kajarra where long-haired sages gathered to discuss philosophy.

In February 1838, Captain T.S. Burt of the Bengal Engineers hears from one of his palanquin bearers about 'the wonders of a place called Khajrao'. Burt, intrigued by the description, travels by palanquin from Chattarpur to Khajuraho to see for himself. His journal published in 1839 gives us an account of what he saw on that historic day and this is the first description we have of Khajuraho. He says that the temples that he saw were all covered under a canopy of trees; that he had to push his way through the undergrowth to get to them. Burt suggests that the temples had been abandoned and left to ruin for seven hundred years, from the time they were built till the day he rediscovered them.

Following Burt, several other visitors, scholars, artists and photographers came to study the temples of Khajuraho. In 1904 the Archaeological Survey of India acquired the land and introduced a systematic conservation programme to protect and restore the temples. The lime plaster on the sculptures was removed and some of the faulty renovation work undertaken by the enthusiastic Raja of Chattarpur was reconstructed. Today all historical monuments and museums in Khajuraho are under the able supervision of the Archaeological Survey of India. In the last decade UNESCO has declared the magnificent monuments of Khajuraho a World Heritage Site.

Kandariya Mahadev and Devi Jagadambi Temples

The Subject Grows Warmer

It was whilst I was on my return trip from Eran to Saugor that I heard, from a palky bearer, of the wonders of the place—Khajrao . . .

The ruins which I went to see lie at some distance from the village, which lies beyond them, and this place I did not see, as a quantity of jungle intercepts the view of it. I was much delighted at the venerable, and picturesque appearance these several old temples presented, as I got within view of them. They reared their sun-burnt tops above the huge trees by which they are surrounded with all the pride of superior height and age. But the chances are, the trees (or jungle rather) will eventually have the best of it . . .

I found in the ruins of Khajrao seven large Diwallas, or Hindoo temples, most beautifully and exquisitely carved as to workmanship, but the sculptor had at times allowed his subject to grow rather warmer than there was any absolute necessity for his doing; indeed, some of the sculptures here were extremely indecent and offensive; which I was at first much surprised to find in temples that are professed to be erected for good purposes, and on account of religion. But the religion of the ancient Hindoos could not have been very chaste if it induced people under the cloak of religion, to design the most disgraceful representation to desecrate their ecclesiastical erections. The palky bearers, however, appeared to take great delight at the sight of those to them very agreeable novelties, which they took good care to point out to all present. I was much struck with the beauty of the inner roofs of the temples, which were circular, and carved in the most elaborate style . . .

There was no masonary, I mean no plaster of any kind, used for the purpose of cementing these slabs to one another, their own weight and position alone being sufficient to give them permanence—a permanence which has lasted for ages, and which would, unless disturbed by the growing of trees or other disturbing causes, sempiternally exist . . .

I noticed a vast quantity of beautiful sculptures of all kinds, to attempt to describe which would exceed the limits of this work, even if, I possessed the means of doing so; but as I do not, and have no sketches from there, I must perforce be excused from inserting any. Having visited several temples, in all seven, of which the names are as follows, I went to take a look at the rest of the wonders of the place.

Captain T.S. Burt.
The Journal of the Asiatic Society of Bengal, 1839.

Kandariya Mahadev Temple, 19th century engraving

Religion

According to the local legend there were once over 85 temples built at Khajuraho, of which 20 are in a fairly good state of preservation. Most of the temples of Khajuraho are Hindu while a few, confined to the Eastern Group, are dedicated to the Jain faith.

The Hindu religion is one of oldest in the world and continues to be practised throughout India. More than a religion, Hinduism is a way of life. Central to the belief is that the Divine manifests itself in innumerable ways. The countless deities of the Hindu pantheon are merely the multitudinous manifestations of the power and energy of the Divine.

Representative of the single phenomenon called Life are Brahma, Vishnu and Shiva. They are not really three male gods but represent the continuous process of creation (Brahma), of preservation of life (Vishnu) and reabsorption or destruction (Shiva). This process of birth, life and death is an unending continuum and cannot be separated, for everything that is born will ultimately die and be reabsorbed by the original creator. In the temples of Khajuraho, this synthesis of Brahma, Vishnu and Shiva is depicted on the lintel above the sanctum and on the walls.

Vishnu and consort

Brahma

Brahma is identified as an old bearded man, as he is the original parent. He carries a sacrificial spoon and a tapering palm leaf book.

Vishnu carries a conch, the symbol of the haunting sound of creation emerging from primeval waters, and disc, the wheel-like weapon that destroys ignorance or evil. Vishnu, as preservor, has nine incarnations in which he appeared to save the universe from annihilation. (*See* Glossary.)

Shiva, as the original creator - destroyer, is represented by the **linga**, an abstract pillar-like form. There are linga images of different kinds in the sanctum of the Kandariya Mahadev, Vishvanath, Matangeshvar, Duladeo and Brahma Temples of Khajuraho. Shiva is also depicted in sculpture in human form, carrying a three-pronged *trishul* or trident in one hand and a snake, the representative of the three worlds, in the other.

Each of the gods are given a consort that represents their *shakti* or energy. There are sculptural figures of the divine couples embracing each other in the niches of the Devi Jagadambi and Chitragupta Temples. Brahma's wife is Saraswati, the goddess of learning and wisdom, Vishnu's wife is Lakshmi, the goddess of prosperity and well-being and Shiva's wife is Parvati. The gods and goddesses are also represented by their animal manifestations. Brahma is said to ride Hansa, the heavenly swan, Vishnu on Garuda, the divine eagle and Shiva on Nandi, the loyal bull. A magnificent specimen of Nandi is sculpted in front of the Vishvanath temple.

Shiva's son **Ganesh** is one of the most popular Hindu deities. He has an elephant head because, according to one myth, his father accidently cut off his original head and replaced it with that of an elephant. An image of Ganesh, the lord of good fortune is found in the first niche on the south side of the Vishvanath and Lakshman Temples. Ganesh is the first deity to be worshipped in all Hindu rituals for, as a remover of obstacles, he sees to the successful completion of every venture.

Adoration of Shiva with garlands

The Temple

The temple is a sacred site, built as a residence for the gods. The temple is therefore built on the principles laid down by the sacred architectural texts called the Shilpa shastra. The temple is designed as a miniature reflection of the divine universe. Most of the temples of Khajuraho face the east, the direction of the rising sun. The temples have a wide platform around them for the *pradakshina* or processional walk around the building in a clockwise direction, beginning from the south side and moving west, north and then finally east and into the doorway. The *pradakshina* is a symbolic circumambulation of the miniature universe on earth.

The exterior walls of the temple are decorated with images of the gods, the manifestations of the divine. The wall has a base that represents the waters and earth that support us all, the main body inhabited by celestial beings in their appropriate places, and above the temple rises the roof, or *shikhara*. The *shikhara* of the Khajuraho temples has a distinctive form, of an inverted cone. The *shikhara* of a mature temple form, as in the Kandariya Mahadev, is built up of miniature *shikhara* clinging to its surface and leading the eye to the pinnacle. The roofs above the porch, *mandap* and *mahamandap*, tend to be pyramidal in shape and the entire profile of a large temple resembles a mountain range, rising up to the sky, like the Himalaya, where the gods are said to reside.

The universal space is protected by guardians and mythical creatures that are also represented on the temple walls. The **Dikpalas** are guardians of the eight cardinal directions. On most of the large and medium-sized temples at Khajuraho the *dikpala* figures are placed on the topmost band of sculptures. The east is guarded by Agni, the lord of Fire. He is represented as a satisfied, pot-bellied god sporting a beard and a halo of fire around him. The southeast is protected by Indra, the lord of the heavens and sky, and he is shown with his mount, the elephant. Yama the lord of death, faces the south, the direction of change. He has fearsome features and often carries a skull. The naked Nirriti, lord of decay, stands to the southwest. Varuna, lord of the ocean faces the west. Vayu of the northwest carries a noose and the pot-bellied Kubera, lord of wealth, is guardian of the north. Isana, the lord protects the northeast side.

The temple also has to be protected from natural calamities and the forces of darkness. The temples of Khajuraho have a host of rampant mythical creatures, some with a lion's head, others with elephant or bird heads on a lion's body. These creatures are seen rearing their gigantic forms and overpowering the aggressive forces. The symbolism of these creatures is profound. The lion stands for physical might and the elephant for wisdom, the two combining to represent an invincible power.

From the crowded external world one enters the hallowed space within the temple. The doorways to the temple are beautifully decorated to welcome the devotee. Within the temple the devotee is taken from the *antarala* (porch) to the *mandap* (hall), and in some of the larger temples to the *mahamandap* or larger hall. The deity is placed in the sanctum called the *garbha griha*, or womb chamber, which is unadorned, dark and calm, like the still centre of the soul. It is from here that the creative energy spreads and radiates beyond the temple walls. The doorway into the sanctum is entered only by the initiated priest.

In Khajuraho the sanctum doorways are profusely decorated with carved panels and rows of sculpture. At the centre of the lintel that bridges the sanctum doorway is the image of the god to whom the temple is dedicated, with the other two gods of the trinity on either side.

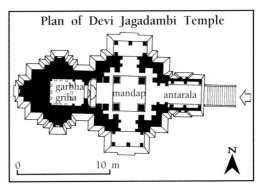

Plan of Devi Jagadambi Temple

A Shiva temple would have Shiva's image in the centre, Brahma to his right and Vishnu to his left. Usually, at the base of the doorway are placed the lovely figures of the goddesses Ganga and Yamuna, representative of the holy rivers that both cleanse and purify us all.

Jain Temples

A Jain temple follows the pattern of its Hindu counterpart. The holiest image in a Jain temple is the figure of the Tirthankara. Vardhamana Mahavir is considered to be the last of the twenty-four Tirthankaras. Parshvanath preceded him and the first of the Tirthankaras was Adhinath, and to these two are dedicated the oldest temples in the Jain Group. The story of Mahavir is exemplary of the principal tenets of Jain philosophy. Mahavir was born into a wealthy royal family. He renounced his earthly inheritance to become an ascetic or hero (*vir*). He eventually achieved the greatest human victory (*mahavir*), the subjugation of material desire and worldly pleasures. From *jina*, the victor, comes the word Jaina or Jain.

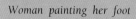

The Story of Khajuraho

Woman painting her foot

Devotees, Maha-Shivratri festival at Khajuraho

The Divine Marriage

The marriage of Shiva,
Matangeshvar Temple

Consumation of the marriage of Shiva and Parvati

THE STORY OF KHAJURAHO

Khajuraho is famous for its remarkable temples and exquisite sculpture and equally infamous for its erotic masterpieces. It was the meaning of these erotic sculptures, boldly placed in a central position on the side of the large temples, that has been the centre of academic debate over the past hundred years. Historians have suggested that Khajuraho represents a decadent phase of history where morals and values had fallen so low that they even depicted sexual intercourse on temple walls. Others believed that the temples were built for a Tantric sect who practiced esoteric rituals. Yet others opined that the erotic sculptures of Khajuraho are a visual illustration of the Kamasutra, the ancient text on the science of love-making, and that the temples were offering the devotees free sex-education. Many people reacted with prudish horror, others with embarrassed amusement.

My own recent research suggests that the erotic sculpture, and indeed the entire temple scheme, of Khajuraho is founded on a deeply religious ritual and philosophic vision, rather than any pornographic intent, as I shall attempt to outline below.

There is a profound philosophic myth about the divine marriage of Shiva and Parvati. Shiva, an ascetic, refused to marry; Parvati the gorgeous female goddess wished only to marry Shiva. Their union was necessary for the creation and protection of the universe. The gods planned to marry these two cosmic powers and sent Kamadev, the Hindu Cupid, the lord of desire, to strike Shiva with his deadly arrows. When Shiva was thus disturbed, he roared with anger, opened his third eye and reduced Kamadev to ashes. At that moment the earth opened up and a linga of Shiva emerged, marking the event of the destruction of Kamadev, the cause of all human suffering. It is believed that the gigantic linga in the Matangeshvar Temple in Khajuraho marks this great event, in which Shiva reveals to us that only with the subjugation of transient, worldly desires can one gain eternal life and everlasting joy.

However, Shiva had fallen in love with Parvati and decided to marry her for the perpetuation of the universe. The date was fixed and all the gods along with their consorts were invited to partake in this greatest cosmic event. Parvati's father invited the architect of the gods to build beautiful mansions for the gods to live in when they attended the wedding festivities.

The divine bridegroom's wedding party set off together in a long, awesome procession heralded by celestial musicians, while others showered flowers and garlands from the skies.

Every year, at the Maha-Shivratri festival, the village of Khajuraho celebrates the wedding of Shiva and Parvati. The wedding procession with an image of the divine couple is taken through the streets heralded by a band of musicians and flag-bearers. The walls of the Parshvanath and the Duladeo Temples commemorate the event when the gods and their consorts assembled for the wedding, with a narrow band of sculpture above depicting the celestial musicians and garland carriers.

The next part of the myth describes how, when the marriage procession arrived, all the women of the city left whatever they were doing to catch a glimpse of the Divine Bridegroom, Shiva. There was a woman feeding her baby, another applying eye make-up, one painting her feet, another had undressed, yet another was bathing, one washing her hair, one making love to her partner. Without exception, they stopped whatever they were doing to see the tumultuous wedding procession pass by.

This section of the myth has been interpreted in the bands of sculptures on the temple walls. There are several depictions of all these women, some half turning, some still engrossed in their mundane activity, as yet unaware of the divine presence of the gods in their midst. It is in these graceful, sensuous female figures of Khajuraho that the artist describes that moment frozen in time when an individual realizes the presence of god. It is a moment of divine inspiration, a moment of unselfconscious awareness.

In the Matangeshvar Temple on the night of Maha-Shivratri the wedding ceremony of Shiva and Parvati is conducted with all the accompanying human marriage ritual. The ceremony lasts the entire night, the one time in the year when in Khajuraho both myth and reality blend together in one harmonious whole.

The myth then relates that after the formal ceremonies Shiva and Parvati retired to spend time together. We are told, in the Shiva Purana text, that Shiva and Parvati made love for a thousand god years. Soon the gods became worried and had to disturb the divine couple and remind them of their role in the preservation of the universe.

It is the divine union of Shiva and Parvati that is depicted in the central panel between the balconies of the Kandariya Mahadev, Lakshman and Vishvanath Temples. It is the embracing images of the gods in the Devi Jagadambi and the Chitragupta Temples that remind us that it is this cosmic union that makes the world go round.

WHAT TO SEE IN KHAJURAHO

A lot depends on when you see the monuments at Khajuraho, the season and climate. The grand temples are always dignified and majestic, but the sensuous sculptures are transformed every minute of the day and night, at dawn, in harsh daylight and in the blazing colours of the sunset. There are over twenty temples to be seen at Khajuraho, each one different and unique.

When the British officer Alexander Cunningham visited Khajuraho in 1852 he noticed that the temples were clustered in groups around the village. He divided the plan of Khajuraho into directional areas and referred to the temples within them as the **Western Group of Temples**, the **Eastern Group**, and this nomenclature continues to this day. The Western Group of Temples lies on the main Bamitha to Rajnagar road, just north of the Shiv Sagar tank. Here you will find the largest and finest examples of Chandella Hindu architecture and sculpture. To the southwest of the Shiv Sagar tank are the more ancient ruins of the Chausat Yogini and the Lalguan Mahadev shrines.

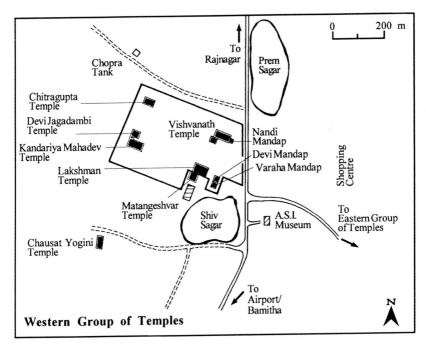

Western Group of Temples

The village of Khajuraho lies a kilometre to the east of the Western Group of Temples. The village has grown over the centuries around a small tank known as the Khajur Sagar. On the east bank and beside the reservoir are the small Hindu Brahma, Javari and Vamana Temples. Past the village, in a south-easterly direction, is a large enclosure with Jain temples and a museum. In this complex the Parshvanath and the Adhinath Temples belong to the Chandella period, while the others have been reconstructed in subsequent centuries by putting together pillars, sculptures and doorways of older shrines.

A turning off the main path to the Jain Temple complex, moving southward, is the Hindu Duladeo Temple beside the Khuddar stream. Another very beautiful temple is Chaturbhuj which is further south on the way to Khajuraho airport.

Shiv Sagar Tank

The Shiv Sagar lies west of the main Bamitha Rajnagar road. Shiv Sagar, the Ocean of Shiva, is used for ritual and ceremonial purposes. Villagers and pilgrims come to the tank to bathe and purify themselves before they enter the temples. Three sides of the tank have been reinforced with embankments, with stairs on the east side leading down to the tank. There are little peddle boats available on hire for 'boating' on the Shiv Sagar. On the north side of the Shiv Sagar is a long white building which is the palace of the Maharaja of Chattarpur. Behind it the upper sections of the Western Group of Temples are visible. The tank is fed by annual monsoons and one can always tell from the water level whether or not Khajuraho has received adequate rainfall during the previous year.

Chausat Yogini Temple

This temple is dated to the ninth century and is the oldest shrine in Khajuraho. It is an intriguing structure built of large, solid granite blocks set on a natural outcrop (about 5.5 metres high). A dirt track along the southeast side of the Shiv Sagar, past the fields, leads to this rarely visited shrine. Chausat Yogini refers to the 64 (*chausat*) *yoginis* or manifestations of the goddess. The temple is approached by a flight of stairs on the north side which opens out into a huge open rectangular courtyard (31 by 18 metres). Along the boundary wall of the courtyard are the remains of 64 tiny one-roomed shrines in which stood the images of the goddesses. The shrines are empty now and the three images found here in the 19th century are kept in the museum. In the region of central and northern India there were once a number of *yogini* shrines where the mother goddess was worshipped. Royal families appealed to these awesome female powers for victory in battle, for human and territorial conquest. It is said that the goddesses had to be appeased with blood sacrifices and similar gifts before she bestowed her favours. One can imagine that the early founders of the Chandella dynasty had received such favours from the Chausat Yoginis which enabled them to expand their empire. Perhaps it was then that they decided to honour her by making Khajuraho a sacred city of temples.

Matangeshvar Temple

North of the Shiv Sagar is a line of shops and a path that leads to the only temple in Khajuraho which is still in active worship. Throughout the year the local villagers and tourists are invited to the daily evening *arti* or prayers. On Shiv-ratri and other important festivals thousands of people come from neighbouring villages to pay homage to Shiva. It is then that the pathway and stairs of the temple throng with people dressed in colourful clothes, all singing the praises of Shiva.

The path to the temple forms the boundary of the Western Group of Temples. The winding path leads to the entrance where you must take off your shoes at the bottom of the stairs. Here you will meet sweet little flower girls waiting to sell garlands to visitors, not as personal adornment but as offerings to the Matangeshvar Temple.

The temple is built on a high platform three metres off the ground. At the top of the steep stairway is a lovely image of a seated Ganesh to whom the first offerings are made. The Matangeshvar Temple is square in plan, though three balconies protrude out of the south, west and northern sides, and there is a broad platform for *pradakshina* or circumambulation. There are no figurative decorations on the exterior walls except in the niches on the cardinal sides. The square temple is surmounted by a high pyramidal roof made up of distinct horizontal levels. Above is a ribbed, circular *amalaka* on which stands a gilded *kalash*, the symbolic pot of ambrosia, the nectar of immortality. The gilded *kalash* was a gift of the late Maharaja of Chattarpur who was a patron of this temple.

The entrance to the temple is from the east. As you approach the steep stairway, the modern additions to the temple become visible; the wall-clock, the picture of Shiva the ascetic, the wooden door and the adjacent stairway. Within the sanctum is a cross-shaped room entirely dominated by a huge 2.5 metre stone linga rising out of an enormous stone pedestal (6.38 metres in diametre). This image is the centre of worship in Khajuraho today. One has to move in a clockwise direction, in single file, around the pedestal and climb the stairs to reach the top. On the pedestal, or *yoni*, sits the priest who will offer prayers on your behalf for a few rupees placed in the tray before him. Above the linga is a wonderful broad corbelled stone roof that descends in circular waves till it meets the supporting side walls. Most devotees enter the temple, make offerings of flowers and water to the linga, which they hug and touch with endearing affection, as if to embrace the power of Shiva, the creator-destroyer.

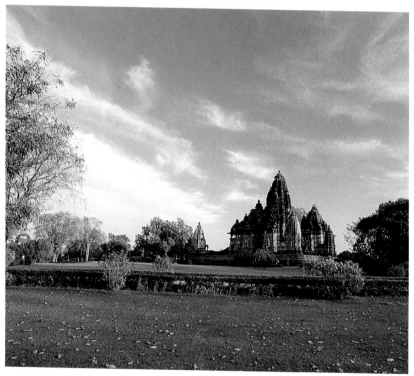

Lakshman Temple

The Temples

WESTERN GROUP OF TEMPLES

On the main road, beside the path leading to the Matangeshvar Temple is the A.S.I counter where you must purchase a ticket to visit the temples in this complex and the museum on the opposite side. A boundary wall surrounds and protects the temples within this large rectangular complex and there is only one entry point (see page 33 Plan of the Western Group of Temples). Here at the Western Group you will see some of the most sensational temples in the world.

Devi Mandap

Opposite the large Lakshman Temple are two small shrines. The one directly opposite is called Devi Mandap, its cemented peaked roof an indication that it has been renovated during the last century.

Varaha Mandap

This open pavilion stands to the south of the Devi shrine on a high platform. The *mandap* stands elevated above the ground with 14 short pillars that support the high pyramidal roof capped with an *amalaka* and *kalash*.

As you ascend the stairs and enter, the beauty of this little pavilion become evident. A low parapet wall forms the side of the *mandap*, and here you can sit on the soft smoothened stone and admire the image of Varaha. Directly under the pyramidal roof stands an enormous monolithic image of the Varaha, the boar incarnation of Vishnu, lord of preservation. The image is made out of a single block of sandstone that measures 2.6 metres long and 1.7 metres high. The stone shines like burnished metal and is one of the most unusual sculptures of Khajuraho. According to Hindu mythology there was a time when the earth was engulfed by primeval floods. Vishnu assumed the form of gigantic cosmic boar and divided the waters and lifted the earth goddess Bhudevi out of their foreboding depths. As Varaha carried the gentle earth out of the waters, on his triumphant back rode the pantheon of gods celebrating the return of the earth to safety. This powerful image of Varaha represents this cosmic event. Varaha stands firm on all four feet, and near his front feet are the remains of a lovely pair of female feet where once stood the figure of the graceful earth goddess. The all-conquering

Varaha towers over a long curvaceous snake and water deities. Along his massive body are neat rows portraying 674 miniature figures of gods and goddesses. Clinging to him are the images of the holy rivers Ganga and Yamuna, and on his face are the nine planets to emphasize that Vishnu saved the entire universe from total annihilation. There are many images of the Varaha in Khajuraho, in the Devi Jagadambi Temple (south side lower niche) and also in the A.S.I. museum, but in both these cases Varaha appears as a gigantic superman with a boar head tenderly carrying the earth goddess on his arm.

Lakshman Temple

This striking temple stands facing the Varaha and Devi *mandaps*. It is one of the three largest temples of Khajuraho and the Western Group and is considered to be the earliest (*c*. AD 954) to have been built by the Chandella rulers.

The temple faces the east and is dedicated to Vishnu, though it goes by a rather inappropriate name of Lakshman, the brother of Ram, the hero

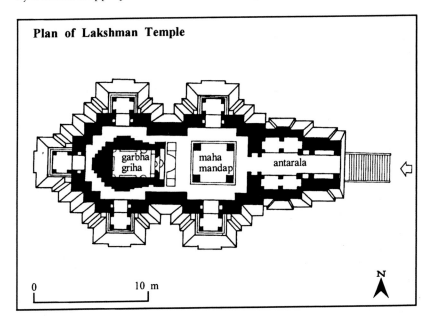

Plan of Lakshman Temple

garbha griha

maha mandap

antarala

0   10 m

N

king of the epic poem Ramayana. The temple is as tall as it is long, measuring approximately 25.9 metres in length. It is raised on a high platform which also has some interesting sculptures (royal processions, court scenes) that you can see before ascending the temple stairs. Moving always around a temple in a clockwise direction (in *pradakshina* with the right shoulder nearest the temple wall), the band of sculptures unfold like an never-ending picture scroll. Along the narrow southeast side passage are erotic panels of sexual rituals: of a man engaged in intercourse with a horse, a regal lord being fanned by a female attendant and other court scenes. There is a lively scene of musicians, a child dancing before the king, a hunting incident in which a wounded deer is being mourned by its fawn as the hunter kneels with his bow and arrow, one of a hunter on horseback pursuing his hapless prey. The remainder of the panel, as it weaves around the Lakshman Temple, depicts caparisoned horses and riders, warring elephants and processions of soldiers.

The Lakshman Temple stands like a giant mountain of stone at the centre, and is unique in Khajuraho for its four subsidiary shrines at the four corners of its rectangular platform. Each subsidiary shrine has a little porch, an ornamental conical *shikhara* and bands of sculpture along the exterior walls.

Once again you must walk in *pradakshina* around the Lakshman Temple to see the abundance of sculptural masterpieces on its outer walls. Starting on the south side you will see that the exterior temple wall is divided into several bands, the lowest, the *adhishthana*, is the base of the temple. The Lakshman Temple is the only one with a row of elephants that peep out of the base as if they are carrying the weight of the stone universe on their stable shoulders. Between the elephants are warriors protecting the temple: on the north side one elephant has forsaken his duty and naughtily gazes

Lady having her bath, Lakshman Temple

at a couple making love. Above the elephants, the moulded *adhishthana* has flower and leaf motifs, a narrow panel depicting court life and erotic scenes. This tall base of the temple is punctuated by ornamental niches, with an adorable figure of dancing Ganesh in the first followed by images of the seven principal male deities of the Hindu Pantheon and ending on the north side with a gorgeous image of the goddess.

Above the *adhishthana* are two bands of figurative sculptures that wind in and around the projections and corners of the temple. It is estimated that there are over 230 figurative sculptures on these bands and each band is about a metre high. There are images of the *dikpalas* placed at and facing the directions that they protect. One band has figures of Vishnu while another has those of Shiva. Beside the deities are the voluptuous figures of women, each engaged in some worldly activity before she realizes the presence of the divine surrounding her. These figures, which have earned Khajuraho its fame, are exquisite portrayals of women attired in traditional costume, flimsy fine textiles wound around the waist while the torso and arms and neck are adorned only in jewellery. There are ladies applying make-up, taking off their clothes, gazing into a mirror. On the western corner, before you turn north, is a seductive woman scrubbing her arched back (*See* page 43). Beside her are two women with their backs turned to the audience watering a holy plant, at the corner is an elegant young woman who has lifted up her foot that is being inspected by an attendant carrying a satchel.

The large erotic sculptures adorning the main body of the temple are placed, as in all the other temples in Khajuraho, on the south and north sides, between the two balconies. On the south side (also seen from the staircase of the Matangeshvar Temple) the top panel depicts a bearded god, identified as Agni; beneath is the figure of the divine bridegroom walking in procession accompanied by musicians. Below, on the lower panel is (my favourite image of) Shiva with his top-knot still secure, embracing his wife Parvati and sharing a passionate kiss that has lasted a thousand god years!

The temple has only one entrance on the east side, set at the top of the stairs. The porch has a pretty *toran* or stone garland above the entrance. Cemented along the porch wall is the Chandella stone inscription found in the vicinity of the temple. The inscription, written in AD 954, records that Yashovarman, the seventh Chandella ruler, constructed a temple to Vishnu and was succeeded by his son Dhangadeva. It is therefore assumed that Lakshman Temple was built just before AD 954 by Yashovarman.

The porch leads into the *mandap*, the *maha-mandap*, the halls of which are illuminated by the filtered light that streams in through the high balconies. It is the four-balcony projections, two on each side, that give the temple its intricate double cross plan. There are images along the ceiling, bracket figures above the faceted pillars of the halls. The sanctum stands behind a very ornamental doorway with carved panels of auspicious motifs. Within the *garbha griha* is the image of Vishnu with two other heads, representing the Varaha and Narasimha incarnations. Around the sanctum is a narrow *pradakshina path*. The exterior wall of the sanctum has a number of panels; on the topmost level are some that depict the life of Krishna, the human incarnation of Vishnu. Here too, enshrined in the niches, are lively images of women engaged in their day-to-day activities standing beside deities and manifestations of the gods. The temple interior remains cool and dark, and the gentle sunlight falls on some of the figures and casts alluring shadows over the others.

Kandariya Mahadev Temple

This is without doubt the largest and most magnificent temple in Khajuraho. The elegant proportions of this building and its sculptural detailing are the most refined examples of the artistic heritage of central India.

Kandariya Mahadev shares its high platform with the small Mahadev shrine and the medium-sized Devi Jagadambi Temple, thereby accentuating its height and grandeur. As far as we know, after the Kandariya Mahadev Temple, the artists of Khajuraho never again attempted to build a structure so high or ornate. The temple measures about 30 metres in length and 20 metres in width. The temple *shikhara* rises 35.3 metres above the ground. From the east side it looks like a huge mountain of stone with a dark cave-like opening set high above the ground. The name Kandariya Mahadev refers also to Shiva, the ascetic who dwells in a mountain cave, lost in meditation. In profile the pyramidal porch, *mandap* roofs and conical *shikhara* look like a range of mountains straining upwards till it meets the sky, or Shiva. The *shikhara* of the Kandariya Mahadev Temple is broad at the base and in a graceful curve grows narrower as it reaches the pinnacle. It is built up of over eighty replica *shikharas* that appear to be clambering up the central tower, giving it both force and momentum on its skyward journey towards divinity.

The plan of the Kandariya Mahadev Temple is similar to the Lakshman and Vishvanath Temples with all the rooms aligned east to west on a central axis. Two balconies project on the south and north sides giving the shape of a double cross. The double cross plan determined that the temple had no straight sides and extended the wall surface to give the artists literally hundreds of metres of wall space to decorate with bands of sculptures.

Perform the *pradakshina* of the temple platform to see the exquisite sculptures on the exterior wall. The *adhishthana* or base of the temple is three metres high and made up of a series of architectural mouldings. On this area of the building there is a narrow band depicting court life. The nine niches around the temple contain images of Ganesh, the seven mother goddesses or Sapta Matrikas. Especially beautiful, but unfortunately badly damaged, is the skeletal form of a dancing Chamunda, and the last niche has the majestic image of Virabhadra. Above the *adhishthana,* the central wall space of the temple is designed with three bands of sculpture, each one a metre high. On the projections of the walls are the figures of the deities; principally of Shiva attired as a bridegroom. Beside him are lovely figures of women engaged in everyday activities. On the southeast projection a woman plays with a ball, another stretches her love-tired limbs, another gazes into a mirror. The erotic panels on all three bands of the south and north sides are exceptional in the Kandariya Mahadev Temple.

Kandariya Mahadev and Devi Jagadambi Temples

On the south side the couples are kissing, their bodies entwined in such perfect union that one can cannot tell the arms and legs of one partner apart from the other. The stances of love making scenes on the north side are more elaborate, often acrobatic and symbolic.

The darker recesses of the wall surface are inhabited by protective creatures, mythical beings fighting the forces of evil and *naginis*, serpent queens folding their hands in prayer and blessing. High above these bands of sculpture the *shikhara* rises toward the sky, towering and dwarfing the human beings below. The play of sunlight over the wall surface creates a rippling effect, casting deep shadows in some areas and bathing others and the sculpture within them in pure light. The design of the temple is therefore entirely symbolic of spiritual progress which is understood as the movement from the mundane to the sacred, from the darkness of ignorance to the eternal light of wisdom.

The entrance to the temple is to the east, and a flight of stairs elevates you high above the ground. The porch has an exceptionally beautiful entrance *toran*. The *toran* is designed like a garland of flowers strung across the doorway to make your entrance both auspicious and hallowed. The garland has been carved out of a single stone and draped with loops from one side of the doorway to the other. The *toran* stems out of the mouths of *makaras*, ever-watchful mythical crocodiles, and within the folds of the garland are tiny flying nymphs who seem to be carrying it across the heavens. Within the temple is the porch (the *mandap* and *maha-mandap*), the inner *pradakshina* path around the sanctum, and every section of these walls is covered with sculptures. A large temple like the Kandariya Mahadev is estimated to have over 870 large sculptures on its exterior and interior walls, each one about metre high.

Even the inner roofs of the porch and *mandap* are worthy of admiration and are created like great upside down pools with flower and leaf motifs. The doorway of the sanctum is profusely decorated with narrow panels of images. The central lintel carries the seated figure of Shiva holding a trident and snake, Vishnu is seated to his left and Brahma to the right. Within the dark, unadorned *garbha griha* or womb chamber stands the creative symbol of Shiva, the linga.

Mahadev Shrine

Between the Kandariya Mahadev and the Devi Jagadambi Temples is a small shrine whose purpose is difficult to ascertain. It is called the **Mahadev**

Sculptured interior, Vishvanath Temple

Mahadev Shrine, Devi Jagadambi and Chitragupta Temples

Shrine and consists of a small open-pillared porch and sanctum. The structure has suffered further through renovations during the last century. A figure of the rampant lion fighting with a kneeling figure, presumed to be the emblem of the Chandellas, has for some reason been installed in the porch. There are two similar rampant lion figures on the platform of the Kandariya Mahadev and Devi Temples.

Devi Jagadambi Temple

This is much smaller than the magnificent Kandariya Mahadev Temple. It has a cross plan with only one set of balconies, only one *mandap* and no inner *pradakshina patha*. However, the Devi Jagadambi Temple has some of the loveliest sculptures in Khajuraho, and because of its medium height most of them are easily visible. There are wonderful representations of the *dikpalas* in their rightful places, the awesome Yama and Nirriti on the south and southwest sides are especially noteworthy. The little niches on the south, west and north sides have endearing images of Vishnu, Shiva and Brahma embracing their consorts. The south side lower niche has an image of Varaha, depicted with a human body and a boar head, emerging from the primeval waters carrying the earth goddess Bhudevi on his arm. She has placed her hand affectionately on his snout as if to pat the boar and thank him for rescuing her.

Apart from the normal repertoire of female figures applying make-up and preening themselves, there are a number of depictions of lovers embracing and these are tucked away in the recesses and shadows of the temple. It is as if the Devi Jagadambi and the Chitragupta Temples were especially assigned to honour love and conjugal harmony, with figures of the divine couples and others depicting every mood of love. A recess on the south side depicts a woman who climbed upon her standing lover, 'as a creeper climbs a tree' to kiss him fervently. On the west side, top row, is a mischievous woman tugging at her lover's beard. There are several such depictions and each visitor soon identifies his or her favourite masterpiece.

On the west side are two of my favourite sculptures, one depicting a woman with her beautiful back turned to the onlooker. She is preoccupied in gazing at her beauty in the mirror, her scarf falling over her shoulder most provocatively. Near her is another seductive woman with a beautiful figure. This is a depiction of the verse in the Shiv Purana which describes a woman who had taken off her clothes to have a bath. When she heard the tumultuous sound of Shiva's wedding procession she came running out to see her lord, unaware that her clothes had not been adjusted properly. Her clothes reveal her naked stomach, her pubic hair, and flow over her slim limbs leaving only her necklaces nestling between her breasts.

Inside the temple the porch and *mandap* leads straight to the sanctum. Here stands a large image, possibly not the original one, representing Devi Jagadambi, goddess of the entire universe.

Chitragupta Temple

Situated a few metres north of the Devi Jagadambi Temple, the Chitragputa Temple is almost identical in plan and size. The temple is 22 metres in length and 13 metres in breadth. Unfortunately, as the temple was renovated under the enthusiastic, but not very scientific stewardship of the Maharaja of Chattarpur, the porch and *mandap* bear conspicuous scars. Within the temple sanctum is the figure of Surya, the sun god to whom the temple is dedicated. Framed by an elaborate carved doorway stands this central figure. He is always shown riding the chariot of the sun which travels non-stop through the sky. His chariot has seven horses, shown at the base of the statue, and in his two hands he once carried lotus flowers that blossom only in the light of the sun. He is depicted, in Hindu iconography, wearing high boots, the only Hindu god to do so; the exception a concession to his 'hot' chariot and the nature of his work!

The exterior wall of the temple also has some fine sculptures. The niche figures portray divine couples. There are a number of other figures that must be seen. On the south wall is a couple embracing. The woman's graceful naked back pulsates with life, while her partner's fingers can be seen gently removing the rest of her clothes. On the west and north side walls there are other equally sensuous figures of couples caressing each other, forgetful of everything as they kiss.

On the north side, lost in the shadows of a recess, is the celebrated scene of Shiva and Parvati's marriage. He holds her right hand in his and Parvati shyly glaces at Shiva, her handsome partner. Beside the divine couple are their *vahan*s Nandi, the bull and Parvati's lion smiling sweetly. This entire temple, like the Devi Jagadambi is full of the joys of sexual union; happy couples engaged in making love for eternity.

Walking back eastward along the path one can see the small damaged **Parvati Temple** with a Chandella temple doorway now exposed to the sunlight. Beside it is an unrelated 19th century whitewashed building that remains closed. The path leads to the third large monumental temple of the Western Group, the Vishvanath Temple and its auxiliary Nandi Mandap. The Vishvanath Temple, like all the others in Khajuraho has its own distinctive character, stylistic features and sculptural masterpieces.

Nandi Mandap

On the northeastern corner of the Western Group of Temples stands a long high platform with the Vishvanath Temple and the Nandi Mandap. Access to the temple is from the south side and at the base of the stairs, leading up to the platform are two lovely elephants. Being partial to elephants, I find these sculptures especially charming. The elephants have been decorated with necklaces of bells and chains, and carry on their backs their mahouts or elephant drivers. One elephant is depicted trampling and hurling a man while his little mahout hides his face in horror.

The Nandi pavilion is not dissimilar to the Varaha Mandap. It consists of a high base (with elephants carrying the building, as in the Lakshman Temple), above which are pillars that support an enormous pyramidal roof. The roof is made up of well-defined horizontal layers, and right on top is the *amalaka* and the *kalash*. The proportions of the Nandi Mandap are larger than those of the Varaha Mandap and serve as an integral part of the main temple design. Within the open pavilion is one of the most endearing images of Nandi, the bull companion of Shiva, to be found anywhere in India. The loyal vehicle

Nandi

of Shiva is called Nandi or happiness, denoting the peaceful joy that comes to anyone who put their absolute faith in Shiva. This Nandi is carved out of sandstone and, like the Varaha figure, it too gleams like burnished metal. The statue has been carved out of a single block of sandstone measuring 2.19 metres from snout to tail and 1.8 metres high. Nandi is seated demurely with his large bulk elegantly placed on a pedestal, his tail tucked beside him. Nandi sits in an attitude that is composed and calm, a lesson to us all, gazing fondly at the Vishvanath Temple where his master resides. Around the *mandap* is a parapet wall which has been fashioned like a stone bench, and is a wonderful place to sit, ruminate and stare. To gaze at the Dantla hills of Khajuraho to the east, or into the sunset over the Western Group and watch the world go by.

Vishvanath Temple

It follows the same plan as the other two large Lakshman and the Kandariya Mahadev Temples. It is about the same size as the Lakshman Temple 26.5 metres long and 17.6 metres wide with a porch (*ardhamandap*), *mandap*, *maha-mandap*, *antarala*, inner *pradakshina patha* and *garbha griha*.

Profile of Vishvanath Temple

The platform of the Vishvanath Temple bears the remains of two subsidiary shrines, and like the Lakshman may once have had the same five temple plan with four small shrines at the corners of the rectangular platform. The exterior wall of the temple consists of a high *adhishthana* with moulded details, narrow narrative panels and flower-leaf motifs. The nine niches carry the manifestations of the image within the sanctum and a lovely dancing Ganesh graces the first niche on the south side. Above the *adhishthana* are three bands of figurative sculptures with the familiar motifs of the preoccupied ladies, deities and *vyalas* (protective mythical beings). The south and north sides, between the balconies, portray on all three bands erotic couples kissing, fondling and making love in a variety of different positions. Beside them are beautiful, though slightly damaged figures of a woman applying kohl to her eye, another has just washed her hair and a third is anointing and cooling her foot with red henna. The artist has captured these graceful ladies as they are about to move and frozen them in time. Their images immortalize the moment of spiritual realization and wonder.

All the rooms within the temple are placed on a central axis facing eastwest. Above the porch, on the central lintel, is a glorious sculpture of Shiva seated with his divine consort on his lap, and it is to this blissful union that the temple appears to be dedicated.

Inside, on the porch wall is the stone inscription discovered by Captain Burt in 1838. There are two inscriptions that have been plastered over the wall (in this century) and they are written in Sanskrit, one a historical copy of the other. The longer one is the original and states that it was engraved in AD 1002, the time of Dhangadeva, the eighth Chandella ruler. It describes the long genealogy of the Chandella rulers and the wondrous reign of Dhangadeva, also recording that he built a great temple and consecrated it to Shiva, installing within it an emerald and stone linga. Could this be the temple built by Dhangadeva ? Secondly, we may ask, where is the emerald linga?

The *mandap, maha-mandap* and *antarala* are designed with faceted pillars, images in niches, elaborately carved bracket figures (many unfortunately missing) that soar up to support the ornate roof. The shadowy *pradakshina patha* takes you around the sanctum, the walls profusely carved with female figures, deities and *vyalas*. Within the embellished sanctum doorway stands the Shiva linga.

From a distance (either the platform of the whitewashed monstrosity or the pathway to the Vishvanath Temple) one can appreciate the ingenuity of the Khajuraho temple design. The Vishvanath Temple profile reveals that the purpose of the balconies is to create a double cross and an undulating ground plan that does not even hint at monotony. The balconies also provide light and ventilation to the inner *mandaps*. From the outside, as light streams through the balcony openings, they appear to hoist the upper levels, the roofs and *shikhara*, off the base, making the whole temple seem weightless as if it were floating in space.

Another remarkable architectural achievement of the design is the interplay of opposites. There is a balance achieved in the play of macro and the micro, the monumental and the subtlest detail, of light and shadows, of horizontals and verticals. The sculptural bands accentuate the earth-bound horizontals of the building while the recesses and projections steer the temple skyward. In bringing together these opposites the artists have succeeded in creating a sense of perfect balance, controlled equilibrium and creative harmony. This harmony is one of the highest canons of art and has been fully realized in the architecture and sculpture of Khajuraho.

The Kiss, Lakshman Temple

(Opposite page) Village fair held during Maha-Shivratri

Village houses of Khajuraho

Sacred groves of antiquity

March 3rd.—Early in the morning the king left Rajnuggur to celebrate the Holi at some temples which are three miles distant. We started on the elephant, and found the road crowded with pilgrims on their way to the fair, which was nearly at an end. Amongst them I recognised types of all the provinces of Northern and Central India—Brahmins of the Ganges, Bengalees, Rajpoots, Jats, and others, some of them making the great Hurdwar pilgrimage and coming from the most distant regions of the Deccan. The pilgrim is nearly always accompanied by his family: a donkey or a half-starved horse carries the old people and the heavy luggage; the women and children carry articles of household use; and the pilgrim alone walks unencumbered, in all his dignity as head of the family.

We soon come in sight of the long line of royal tents, close to which was our own encampment. About a gunshot off, the crowd was amusing itself beneath the shadow. of large trees, above the thick foliage of which rose the summits of the temples, the objects of the pilgrimage . . .

Holica is no longer the Goddess of Spring, impersonating the reawakening of the Indian Nature: she is a female demon, typifying the most shameless vice, who, springing from the head of Mahadeva, creates discord in Merou, the Brahmin Olympus. She even obtains the mastery over Brahma and Indra, whom she inveigles into the most reckless adventures. The gods supplicate her in vain to cease her wiles, but she only makes sport of their entreaties. At last Brahma confers upon her twenty-four titles of honour, such as Trigita and Dhoundia; and Holica, overcome with joy, sets them at liberty, after having exacted from them an oath that they would celebrate her name each year by festivals and wild saturnalia.

*Thus, as we passed within sight of the fair-field on our return
from exploring the temples in the evening, it seemed as if we
were approaching one of those sacred groves known to antiquity,
within the sombre depths of which the most monstrous scenes
were enacted. Countless bonfires, the flames of which shot up
above the trees, were surrounded by seething crowds, whose
shrieks and yells were half drowned by the beating of thousands
of cymbals, gongs, and tom-toms. Women and children were
hurrying across the plain, vociferating hymns in honour of the
terrible Holica; and all around were being perpetrated deeds
which form the crown and glory of this ignoble divinity.*

Louis Rousselet.
India and its Native Princes, 1875

Devi Jagadambi Temple wall, 19th century engraving

EASTERN GROUP OF TEMPLES

Khajuraho Village

A kilometre towards the east from the Western Group of Temples is the Khajur Sagar and the old village of Khajuraho. On one of the paths to the village is a modern whitewashed structure with a large orange-red statue within. The statue is still worshipped but is one of the oldest images to be found in Khajuraho. The image is of Hanuman, the monkey king who assisted Ram (of the Ramayana) through his travails in exile.

The village is lovely and as yet quite unspoilt, but every day the damaging imprints of 'modernization' appear. The old houses are built of slim baked red bricks with tiled, gently sloping roofs. The house is built around a central courtyard which is used for common household activities of washing and drying. The rooms built around the central space are cool with low ceilings and thick whitewashed walls. Occasionally one sees lovely painted motifs along the doorway and windows created by the woman of the house. The village houses are built very close together. The narrow lanes are cobbled, and widen only where two lanes meet or for the community well. Statues and bits of ancient sculpture are still found lying scattered around, supporting a roof or resting against a wall. The children of the village have seen foreign tourists all their lives and speak many languages—English, French or even Japanese—and always ask for a pen, or a rupee.

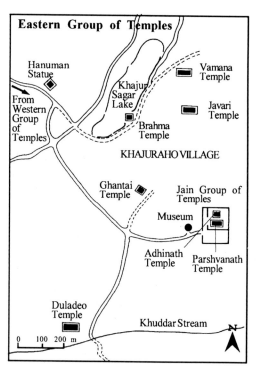

Eastern Group of Temples

Hanuman Statue

From Western Group of Temples

Khajur Sagar Lake

Vamana Temple

Javari Temple

Brahma Temple

KHAJURAHO VILLAGE

Ghantai Temple

Jain Group of Temples

Museum

Adhinath Temple

Parshvanath Temple

Duladeo Temple

Khuddar Stream

0   100   200 m

N

Brahma Temple

On the south end of the Khajur Lake is the first of three Hindu temples. It is a robust little structure that stands on a square platform measuring about six metres. The temple has a simple square plan that consists of only a sanctum and no *mandaps*. The walls of the temple are unadorned with heavy figurative work. The stone lattice windows project a little from three walls, a mere suggestion of the dramatic balconies of the larger temples of the Western Group. The roof, instead of being in the characteristic conical *shikhara* form, is like those above the large temple *mandap*–pyramidal and constructed in clear horizontal levels. The linga inside the temple is quite unique and carries the five manifestations of Shiva (*see* Beyond Khajuraho: Nacchna), a composite image of his multiple powers and potentialities.

The Brahma Temple exemplifies one of the principal problems in studying Khajuraho. When Captain Burt discovered the temples he records that they had been abandoned and left to ruin. Many of the original names of the temples had been forgotten. Today this shrine is called Brahma, but it has a Shiva linga in the sanctum and the lintel above the sanctum door clearly indicates that it once was dedicated to Vishnu!

Javari Temple

Down the path from the Brahma Temple and situated to the east, in the middle of a field, is the small platform on which this temple stands. The name Javari is derived from the one-time owner of the land, or so it is assumed, for there is no Hindu deity bearing this title. The temple is diminutive and its proportions are attractive, measuring 11.88 metres in length and 6.4 metres in breadth. The temple, though substantially renovated, has the characteristic exterior walls lined with bands of sculptures, niches on the cardinal points, but all in miniature form. The dainty roof over the porch grows to meet the pyramidal *mandap* roof and this leads the eye to the elegant *shikhara* above the sanctum.

The temple, dedicated to Vishnu, consists of a long porch entered through a nice stone *toran*. The makara-toran has four decorated loops crowned by a *kirtimukha*. The *mandap* is small as is the inner *garbha griha*. This structure is similar in style to the Chaturbhuj Temple.

Brahma Temple

Javari Temple with Vamana Temple in the background

Vamana Temple

The path from the Brahma Temple leads north to the Vamana Temple enclosure. The temple looks out on to the surrounding fields and every season it has a different aspect, whether against a foreground of a ripening green crop or the golden-yellow harvest. The temple is of medium size and in plan is similar to the Devi Jagadambi and the Chitragupta Temples of the Western Group. Unfortunately the porch of the temple has collapsed, and without it looks a little stunted. It measures 19.1 metres in length and 13.9 metres in breadth (while the Devi Jagadambi is 23.4 metres long and 14.9 metres wide).

The Vamana Temple consists of a *mandap* and *garbha griha* which contains the dwarf image of Vamana, an incarnation of Vishnu. According to the myth, there was once a haughty king and Vishnu assumed the form of a dwarf or Vamana to teach him a lesson. He requested the proud (hence foolish) king for just so much land as he could cover with three strides. The king granted the request and Vishnu took one step and covered the earth, with the second step he strode across the heavens and had nowhere to place his third step. The despotic king realized his mistake, begged forgiveness and requested Vishnu-Vamana to place his third step on his head as a mark of his submission to god.

Around the temple are two bands of sculptures with almost 300 figures, though this is only half the number to be found in any of the larger temples of the Western Group. Here too the sculptural scheme continues with a blend of gods, their consorts, female figures and mythical creatures.

JAIN GROUP OF TEMPLES

Southeast of Khajuraho village, the road ends in front of the complex of Jain Temples. On the way to the Jain complex, at the southern edge of the village and barely visible from the road are the ruins of the **Ghantai Temple**. All that remain are pillars, some with bells (*ghanti*, hence the name) dangling on chains all carved in stone. Cunningham discovered the only Buddhist statue to be found in Khajuraho in the vicinity of the Ghantai Temple.

The Jain Temple complex was recently developed, with shops and a small museum displaying Jain images salvaged from the vicinity. A gateway leads into the enclosed complex, to one side of which is the Dharamshala, the hostel for visiting devotees. To the left is a temple that is in worship, called the Shantinath. This temple is an assemblage of the fragments, pillars and images from older temples and is built around a courtyard. In the central niche is the tall (4.5 metre) image of Adhinath. The path leads to another enclosure within which are two interesting temples.

Parshvanath Temple

This temple is built on a low plinth, unlike the high platforms of all other temples at Khajuraho, which makes it much easier to study the sculptures here. The temple is rectangular in shape with few star-like projections that add so much variety to the other temples of this period. The Parshvanath Temple has a porch on the east side that leads into the *mandap* and sanctum. There is also a projection on the west side, apparently added later, containing a small shrine.

The main exterior wall of the temple is divided into two broad bands with a narrow one above. The narrow panel is composed of wonderful flying nymphs and *gandharva* figures playing musical instruments and showering the assembly of gods below with flowers. The band below is set with images of the gods with their consorts. It's a virtual Who's Who of the Hindu pantheon with every identifiable (and unidentifiable) deity present. On the south side the lowest band has a remarkable representation of Vishnu holding his conch and disc, and embracing his wife Lakshmi. The *dikpalas* stand in position guarding their quarters. There are the usual female figures, one putting kohl in her eye, the other feeding her baby and a third gracefully lifting her foot to paint it with henna. On the north are several lovely ladies, one of whom has raised her foot to put on her ankle bells. Apart from these, the figures of the Parshvanath Temple tend to be a bit heavy, overweight, with circular melon-shaped breasts and thick thighs. Above the bands of sculpture rises the temple *shikhara*. Its rather clumsy heavy appearance indicates that it is either an early experiment, built years before the others (around AD 950), or has been poorly reconstructed during the past two centuries.

The porch entrance has a central image, not unlike the Vishvanath or the Kandariya Mahadev Temple, with Parvati seated on Shiva's knee. The *mandap* and inner *pradakshina patha* are dark and not as well ventilated as the larger temples of the Western Group. Within the sanctum is a highly polished stone image of Parshvanath which, according to Cunningham, was installed in 1860.

Adhinath Temple

Standing beside the Parshvanath temple, on the north side, is this exquisite little temple. The temple exterior has been divided into an *adhishthana*, above which are two rows of sculptures and a narrow band of celestial musicians and garland bearers. The first perception of the figurative art of the Adhinath Temple is that it is so elegant and refined, so different from its heavier, stubbier counterparts in the Parshvanath Temple. The female forms are lithe and supple, twisting their backs to look over their shoulders, their limbs elegant, slim and perfectly proportioned. If any criticism is due it would be that they are more divine than human. They wear intricately woven, patterned costumes, the waist garment held in place with jewel-studded belts, the heavy necklaces set with gems, their arms covered with bangles and feet with ankle bells. Each woman here has a most splendid hairstyle: some wear clips and hair jewellery others wear flowers. To do justice to the sculptures of the Adhinath Temple one needs a pair of binoculars.

The design of the *shikhara* of the temple is no less beautiful. Instead of the usual *shikhara* made up of miniature replica forms, here the tower springs out of the main body of the temple and curves smoothly inward only at the top. The entire surface of the *shikhara* is decorated with abstract patterns of *chaitya* windows and arabesque. The design is carved in low relief, just deep enough to create shadows, the dark and light becoming an integral part of the pattern.

Jain Tirthankara, Museum
(Below) Adhinath Temple wall

Parshvanath Temple
(Below) Adhinath Temple

SOUTHEASTERN GROUP OF TEMPLES

A turning off the main road to or from the Jain complex brings you down a motorable path to this lovely temple alongside the Khuddar stream. The temple looks its best at sunset, when the light illuminates the western end of the temple creating the most dramatic effects.

Duladeo Temple

This temple, judging from a 1904 photograph, was severely damaged; its *shikhara* had all but collapsed and the *mandap* roof caved in, but all this has been renovated and reconstructed now. The temple has a damaged porch and a wide open *mandap* with an amazing circular corbelled inner ceiling. The sanctum has a Shiva linga decorated with many miniature replicas. The dancing figures on the pillars and pilasters of the *mandap* are noteworthy for their vigour and energetic stances.

The temple is also called the Kunwar Math, and along with the term

Dula is associated with the notion of the Bridegroom's temple. The exterior walls have repeated images of the Divine Bridegroom and his consort. The western wall, which is the part of the temple that is better preserved, has three distinct bands of sculpture. The topmost level is decorated with celestial musicians and garland bearers, the next two lower levels have magnificent images of Shiva the Bridegroom, the other deities, mythical creatures; and in the deep recesses are portrayals of lovers and *maithuna* couples. The sculptures of the Duladeo Temple are refined, slim and well-proportioned. The figures, both men and women, wear more jewellery here than in any other temple in Khajuraho.

Duladeo Temple

The plan of the temple is exaggerated and has assumed a star-shape with clear angles, shadowy recesses and clear-cut projections. The *shikhara* begins its upward journey from a transitional base of small *shikharas*, then rises up in a dramatic conical form surrounded by miniature replicas of itself along the sides. This temple is considered by historians to be one of the last monuments to be built in Khajuraho (around AD 1100) and the style of the architecture and sculpture are highly evolved.

Chaturbhuj Temple

This temple stands off the main Khajuraho Airport or Bamitha road. It is approximately three kilometres south of Khajuraho and is approached by a motorable road. The temple stands lonely and serene on a high platform against the backdrop off the Lavanya hills. This is the only important temple in Khajuraho that faces west and it is worth saving your sunset to visit this little shrine. The temple is similar to Javari of the Eastern Group but like all temples in Khajuraho, it too is unique.

The temple has a shallow porch, a little *mandap* surmounted by a peaked roof and a small square *garbha griha* above which rises a tall, slim *shikhara*. The outer walls of the temple are organized into three bands of sculpture and there are a number of unusual niche figures, including the **consort of Narasimha**, on the north side.

Entering the temple one is overpowered by the ornamental doorway and the enormous image within the sanctum. Nowhere in Khajuraho is there a more elegant statue of a deity. Some say the image is a form of Shiva, others say it is Vishnu and yet others believe it is an unusual combination of these two major Hindu deities, as Hari-Hara.

The image is carved out of a single stone and stands 2.75 metres high. The figure stands in a relaxed pose with one leg bent behind resting on the toes. The rendition of the magnificent male torso, slim but firm limbs, the calm expression of the face, dominant chin, large meditative eyes and full lips are breathtaking. At sunset the sun comes streaming in and falls on the figure, lighting it in such a way that it appears to be pulsating with life.

Archaeological Site Musuem

This is a very nice, well-kept museum with a small but interesting collection. The museum stands to the south, on the opposite side of the road from the Shiv Sagar and the Western Group of Temples. The entrance ticket to the museum is the same as the one you have for the Western Group so remember to take it with you. The museum is open from 10am to 5pm every day except Fridays and Government holidays.

The museum is divided into four sections: the central hall, to the left is the hall with Jain sculptures and beyond is the Vaishnava Gallery with images of Vishnu and other deities. On the right hand side of the central hall is a room displaying a general collection of sculptures, followed at the end by the Shaivite Gallery with some extraordinary sculptures. If you want a little more information about the images, their meaning and mythology, turn to the end of this book and match items from the GLOSSARY with the museum captions on the sculptures.

The central hall is dominated by a delightful sculpture of **Dancing Ganesh**. It is a huge (1.8 metre high) carved sandstone masterpiece. Ganesh

is dancing with his arms and legs in vigorous movement, imitating his father Shiva, the cosmic creator—dancer of the universe. In one hand he holds a bowl of sweets for Ganesh who, considering his pot-belly, not surprisingly has a sweet-tooth. In the other hands he carries other emblems. Near his jewelled feet is a little mouse, his vehicle or *vahan*, also accompanying his master in the celebratory dance.

In the Jain gallery are standing and seated peaceful figures of the Tirthankaras, lost in meditation and inspiring a life of non-violence and a frugal existence where human greed has no place.

The Vishnu Gallery has two wonderful images in the western

Dancing Ganesh, Museum

corner. **Vishnu lying on the Serpent couch** dated around the 11 and 12th centuries is a calm and peaceful image, depictings Vishnu the cosmic preserver, lying on the sea of eternity between periods of creation and destruction. Above, is a halo of tiny images representing the nine incarnations of Vishnu. Beside this statue is one of **Varaha**, Vishnu as a half man-half boar that appeared to save the earth goddess from the primeval floods. She is seated on his arm and holds on to Varaha's snout most affectionately.

There are two images of Surya riding on his chariot of the sun drawn by seven horses. In the general gallery, beside the entrance hall, are many statues of women, a hunting scene and one depicting workers carrying blocks of stone as if in the act of constructing a temple of Khajuraho. The central piece is called **King and Queen** and is dated to the 12th century. It is believed that this is one of the rare sculptures depicting the royal patrons of the temples making an offering. One imagines that the King and Queen attended the consecration ceremony when the temples of Khajuraho were completed and sanctified for worship.

In the Shiva Gallery there are two huge images, one of **Parvati** and the other of **Sada Shiva**, both exceptional sculptures. The Shiva image depicts him seated with a linga-like column of seven heads, four feet and eight arms. A charming image of Ganesh seated with his two wives also graces the gallery.

Shiva and Parvati, Museum

Madhya Pradesh

DELHI

RAJASTHAN

Agra

UTTAR
PRADESH

Gwalior
Datia
Jhansi
Orccha

Varanasi

Chanderi

KHAJURAHO
Panna

BIHAR

Sanchi

Bandhavgarh
National Park

Mandu

BHOPAL

Kanha
National Park

GUJARAT

MAHARASHTRA

ORISSA

ANDHRA
PRADESH

Delhi

Bombay

0   250 km

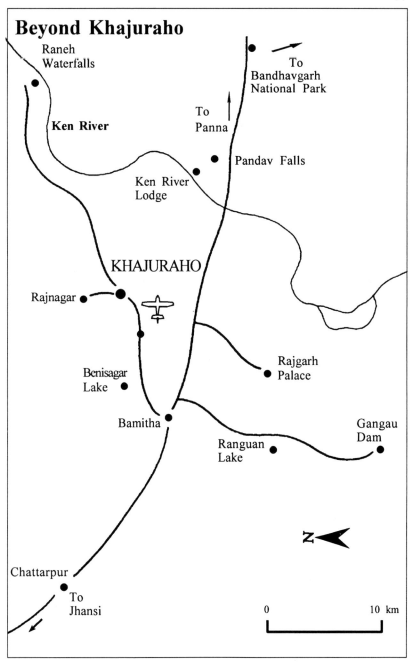

Beyond Khajuraho

BEYOND KHAJURAHO

There are a number of interesting sites to see in and around Khajuraho for both the nature lover and the cultural aesthete. A brief description of some of these sites is given below to whet your appetite and to make your trip to Central India more meaningful. At the end of this section a few suggestions have been provided on HOW TO PLAN YOUR VISIT.

Jhansi

If you are coming to Khajuraho by road or rail, Jhansi is a good starting point. Jhansi is 98 kilometres from Gwalior and 175 kilometres from Khajuraho. It is the most convenient railhead to get to Khajuraho and back to Delhi. Air-conditioned coaches, buses and taxis await incoming trains to ferry travellers to Khajuraho.

Jhansi is better known for its history than for urban aesthetics. In the 19th century the British East India Company, in order to gain control over Indian territory, introduced a law decreeing that when a local ruler had no heir, his state would be annexed. In 1853 the ruler of Jhansi died without an heir and the state was to fall into the hands of the East India Company. Lakshmi Bai, Rani of Jhansi, led a rebellion against this iniquity, fighting bravely to keep her state from falling under foreign control. The British contingent in Jhansi was massacred, but subsequently the British captured Jhansi and the Rani, masquerading as a man, was killed in battle. The valiant Rani of Jhansi and this city associated with her have become the subject of countless heroic ballads, poems and songs.

Two kilometres from the railway station is the old fort and old city. The impressive fort walls, in places 30 metres high, can be seen contouring the granite outcrop above the town. Rather awful painted statues of the Rani of Jhansi riding into battle on horseback, the emblem of this town, are visible all around.

Datia

Datia is on the Gwalior to Jhansi road, 26 kilometres northwest of the city of Jhansi. One has to hire a taxi or take a local bus from Jhansi and plan to spend at least a (very rewarding) half day at Datia.

Corridors of Govind Mandir, Datia

View of Govind Mandir from the tank, Datia

It is a beautiful site built on a natural outcrop and consists of 16th to 17th century fortification walls, palaces and cenotaphs of the region's former Bundelakhandi Rajput ruling family. If unable to visit all the sites, take the short detour off the main Gwalior to Jhansi road that leads to one of the prettiest palaces of Datia.

The main palace, like the one in Orccha, was built by Raja Bir Singh in 1620. The palace overlooks a lake on the south and east side and from the balconies are also visible the remains of the fort, and other palaces and temples of ancient Datia. The many-storeyed palace is called **Govind Mandir**. It is square in plan, with towering walls protecting the inner open courtyard. The high enclosure walls and corners are capped with domes. The commanding entrance doorway to the palace is decorated with carved details, painted motifs and the auspicious image of Ganesh—the elephant - headed Hindu deity, the Remover of Obstacles, the Lord of Good Fortune. Entering the palace through a maze of arched, dark passageways and shadowy doorways one emerges into the sunlit courtyard. The open court is occupied by a smaller, square, many-storeyed building which is linked to the outer courtyard by flying bridges. The entire design of the square within a square and the bridged passageways forms an intricate cruciform plan. As you ascend each floor, the carved pillared passageways lead you from room to room, to screened balconies with views of the lake below and cool royal apartments. Every now and again you can glimpse the remnants of brilliant ceramic tile-work mosaics that once adorned the palace walls. The palace is a playful combination of arches and domes acquired from Islamic architecture, and traditional beams and pillars with ornate brackets.

This palace is one of the best examples of royal, domestic architecture, with a perfect understanding of the Indian climate and the intensity of light. There are rooms that receive the delicate light of dawn, that glow with the blazing sunset; there are cool rooms that never receive direct sunlight and areas that are bathed in light; and in the corridors light and shadows play all day. Both the design and the architectural decoration makes this forlorn palace one of the loveliest in central India.

Orccha

If you are travelling by road from Jhansi to Khajuraho (or back), it is worthwhile making a detour to see the lovely, deserted, 16th century royal capital of Orccha.

Orccha lies 19 kilometres southeast from Jhansi on the Khajuraho road. Taxis are available on hire for a round trip from Jhansi to Orccha and Datia. Accommodation is available at Orccha at the MP Tourism Hotel Sheesh Mahal (Tel: 224). One can spend an entire day picnicking by the pretty river and visiting Orccha's painted palaces, temples and mausoleums. Raja Rudra Pratap chose this exotic site on the loop of the Betwa river and built the fortification walls and citadel. The buildings were completed by his successors. Bir Singh Deo (1605 to 27) was ruler of Orccha during the reign of the Mughal emperor Akbar. Bir Singh sought an alliance with Akbar's son, Prince Salim, later to be known as Emperor Jahangir, and together they plotted and killed Abu'l Fazl one of Akbar's chief ministers. The lovely **Jahangir Mandir** was built by Raja Bir Singh for his friend Jahangir when he visited Orccha. During Jahangir's reign Bir Singh rose to great prominence but fell from grace when he revolted against Jahangir's successor Shah Jahan (the builder of the Taj Mahal in Agra). Bir Singh was defeated by Shah Jahan's son Aurangzeb, destined to become the next Mughal emperor.

There is a lovely little arched bridge that leads to the rocky island on which stand the remains of three palaces. The most beautiful palace in Orccha is **Jahangir Mandir**, square in plan with doorways on its massive fortified exterior. The elaborate entranceway leads into a square courtyard surrounded on four sides by decorated palace rooms, passageways, balconies and pretty windows that offer breathtaking glimpses of the Betwa River.

Raj Mahal, stands to the right of the courtyard. Similar to other royal architecture of the region, the bold, somewhat severe, exterior gives no hint of the opulence and beauty of the interiors.

Rai Praveen Mahal is a two-storeyed brick structure set in the gardens of Anand Mahal. According to legend this delicately proportioned palace was constructed for a lovely poetess and musician who loved Raja Indramani, the ruler of Orccha. She was taken to the Mughal court where, having expressed her loyal, undying love for the ruler of Orccha was permitted by the emperor to return home.

Of the many temples of Orccha there are three that dominate the landscape. **Ram Raja Temple** was originally a palace belonging to Madhukar Singh (who also built Raj Mahal). He had brought to Orccha an image of Ram, an incarnation of Vishnu, the heroic prince of the epic poem Ramayana. The image of Ram was kept in his palace while a new **Chaturbhuj Temple** was being constructed. When the time came, the image refused to be moved and Ram continues to occupy the palace of the king.

Jahangir Mandir, Orccha

Cenotaphs of the Orccha rulers, beside the Betwa river

Painted rooms, Orccha

Vishnu saving an elephant in distress, Orccha

Laxminarayan Temple is connected to Ram Raja Temple by a pathway. The interiors of the temple are ornate, with traces of mural paintings in ochre, red, brown and green mineral hues. The paintings depict religious myths and secular scenes in a lively style characteristic of the region.

Along the Betwa river, south of the palaces, stand the large **cenotaphs** of the Orccha rulers. In the Hindu tradition, the dead are cremated, and the ashes cast into the river. Under Muslim influence, Rajput rulers in western and central India began to build mausoleums for their dead rulers. The design of the cenotaphs is therefore an unhappy and uneasy blend of Mughal tomb styles and local temple architecture.

Jarai Math Temple

The temple stands on the main Jhansi to Khajuraho road (22 kilometres from Jhansi). It is a lovely tenth century temple built within an enclosed courtyard. The structure consists of a square sanctum and towering roof or *shikhara*, and carved details along the temple wall. The doorway to the sanctum and the base of the entrance are profusely decorated with carved panels and the customary images of the purifying river goddesses Ganga and Yamuna (a feature common to all the temples at Khajuraho).

Dhubela Museum

Situated a little off the Jhansi to Khajuraho road, this museum is about 65 kilometres from Khajuraho. It is an old palace set in a lovely forested area beside a lake. The museum houses Hindu sculptures (especially images of Mother Goddesses) found in the region, and weapons and paintings belonging to the Bundelkhand Rajput royal family of the region.

The Dhubela Museum is open from 10 am to 5 pm. It is closed on Mondays and public holidays.

Raneh Waterfalls

The Raneh waterfalls lie 20 kilometres east of Khajuraho, easily accessible by car (if you are up to it, by bicycle). The road leads into a wooded area which opens out to the vast expanse of the Ken river. Gigantic sandstone boulders along the Ken river make this a perfect picnic and sunbathing spot. For the bird-watcher this is also an opportunity to study water fowl in their natural habitat beside the river.

Along a marked pathway you can follow the Ken river as it plunges down gorges. The pink sandstone boulders, sculpted by the water over the centuries, glow like burnished metal in the fading light of the setting sun.

Mahoba

North of Khajuraho, through Rajnagar, are several ancient sites associated with the Chandella rulers who built the magnificent temples of Khajuraho. Mahoba, about 65 kilometres from Khajuraho, is a historic town that was once the capital of the Chandella dynasty.

The town is quite crowded but the remains of Chandella rule are still visible in the ruined fort along the Madan Sagar, a lake that has two sadly neglected temples constructed on little islands in its midst. Near Mahoba is a pretty tank called Rahilya with another ruined temple.

Benisagar Lake

Situated about 11 kilometres down the Khajuraho to Bamitha road, the lake was created when a dam was built across the Khuddar river. It covers an area of over seven square kilometres and is a pleasant picnic spot and suitable for angling and boating.

Ranguan Lake

On the main Bamitha to Panna road there are many lovely, picturesque spots such as Ranguan Lake (25 kilometres from Khajuraho). Take a car and a picnic and relax or fish beside the calm waters of the lake.

Gangau Dam

Also just off the main Bamitha to Panna road, about 34 kilometres from Khajuraho, lies the confluence of the Ken and Simri rivers. The dam site and lake offer an ideal picnic spot to get a bit of sun and relaxation.

Rajgarh Palace

This is one of loveliest sites outside Khajuraho. The deserted palace is visible from the main Bamitha to Panna road. Taking a turning at the village of Chandranagar, the palace is situated about 25 kilometres from Khajuraho at the foot of Maniyagarh Hills. You can visit it en route to the Ken River and Panna National Park.

A wooded hill forms the backdrop of the palace complex. There are ruined palatial apartments along the 35 metre climb up to the palace. The fort-cum-palace, about 150 years old, was built by the Parmar rulers of Chattarpur state who were employees of Rajgarh. The palace is built in the traditional style of the region, and like its counterparts in Orccha and Datia has a defensive exterior that opens into a wide, open courtyard. The apartments and rooms are built along the four sides of this courtyard. There is a splendid array of cool rooms with windows and doorways that capture the tiniest whisp of breeze. From the palace windows and doorways one can view the wonderful Dantla hills of Khajuraho, the flat plains and farmlands and, after a good monsoon, the reservoirs and lakes shimmering with abundant water.

Rajgarh Palace

Ken River

There are several beautiful rivers that rise from the Vindhya hill ranges of central India. One of the prettiest is the Ken or Kiyen. The river flows in a northerly direction until it meets with the holy river Ganges. On the Bamitha to Panna road, there is a large bridge that takes you into Panna district and the Panna National Park.

There are two lovely spots, **Gille's Tree House** and the **Ken River Lodge** where one can drive up (approximately one and a half kilometres off the main road) to the banks of the Ken river. Both sites have wonderful tree houses built on trees that overhang the river. There are rocks and tiny patches of sand where one can paddle, bathe, sunbathe and fish.

Gille's Tree House offers cold drinks and hospitality to picnickers.

Ken River Lodge has four rooms or cottage accommodation and dining facilities. They also organize theme parties and special outings to near-by sites like Panna National Park, Rajgarh Palace, Panna, and excursions to Bandhavgarh National Park. At present, for all bookings for accommodation contact the Manager of the Chandella Hotel, Khajuraho.

Ken River Lodge, on the Ken river

Panna National Park

A range of flat-topped hills rise above the east bank of the Ken river, 40 kilometres from Khajuraho on the Bamitha to Panna road. This area is protected as the Panna National Park and boasts of the last vestiges of the glorious teak forest that once covered so much of the region. The teak forests are magnificent just after the monsoons, and in autumn when great pyramids of white teak flower perfume the atmosphere. In summer the giant teak leaves wither into lacy skeletons and fall, covering the earth with a carpet of many hues. The park is open from November to June, remaining closed through the monsoons in an effort to protect its wildlife.

The park is spread over 546 square kilometres with picturesque gorges, waterfalls and thick teak forests. Only petrol-driven jeeps are permitted within its confines, and on an early morning guided tour, if lucky, you may see the graceful spotted deer or *chital*, black buck, the Indian gazelle, a herd of wild boar; even tiger and panther roam these lovely forests.

Pandav Falls

Up the ghat road, and about a kilometre off the main Bamitha to Panna road is a breathtaking waterfall which, just after the monsoon rains in the months of October and November, is a joy to see. The steep gorge in the hillside brings water from the hilltop cascading down to a great pool below. A flight of steep steps takes you from the car park to the pool where you can picnic and relax. The waterfall gets its name from a local legend that in times gone by the five exiled Pandav brothers of the epic poem Mahabharata visited this region. Remains of caves and shrines that commemorate this legend can be seen around the pool below.

Panna

This historical city is 45 kilometres away from Khajuraho. It is the district headquarters and was once the capital town of the Bundella kingdom of Central India. Panna town is celebrated for its temples built by the local rulers and their queens. They are of particular interest as many of the temples are still in worship and draw large crowds in festival time. There are tours from Khajuraho to Panna via Panna National Park.

Padmavati Devi Temple is one of the oldest in Panna, and it is from this goddess that the name of the town is said to have been derived. **Prannath Temple** is well-known to all the followers of Mahatmati Prannathji's philososphy. The **Jugal Kishoreji Temple** is one of the most important temples at Panna, and is dedicated to Krishna. Legend has it that the image was destined for Orccha but wished to be installed in the sacred city of Panna. There is a very famous temple in Puri, in eastern India, dedicated to Krishna and a similar deity is enshrined in the **Jagannath Swami Temple** in Panna. Each year a huge *rath-yatra* or chariot festival is organized, and the deity is placed in a chariot that is drawn through the streets in procession by hundreds of pilrgims and devotees. The **Baldeoji Temple** is one of the most unusual temples in central India. It is built in a strange hybrid style, a mixture of St Paul's Cathedral in Rome and a 19th century Hindu temple.

There is only limited accommodation available at Panna in the Circuit House and Indian-style privately owned hotels.

Panna Diamond Mines

Till 1725, when diamonds were discovered in South Africa and Brazil, India was the only known diamond-producing country. Rulers the world over coveted the Indian diamond from Golconda (Deccan, India) and Panna for their regal jewellery and crowns.

In Panna the diamonds are found either on the surface, requiring no heavy machinery or mining, or within stratified deposits in the soil.

About 56 kilometres away from Khajuraho and 20 kilometres south of Panna are the only mechanized diamond mines. They are situated at Majhgawan, which is controlled by the Diamond Mining Project of the National Mineral Development Corporation Ltd. (A Government of India Undertaking). These mines can be visited from 9am to 11am even without prior permission. All foreign visitors are required to show their passports for entry into the mining area.

Ajaygarh

This historic fort is perched on a high plateau about 80 kilometres from Khajuraho (via Panna). It was the capital of the Chandellas during its declining years.

A steep climb along a goat track up the hillside takes you through wooded areas. The fort walls hug the rim of the plateau, and within the fort are remains of palaces, temples and tanks. The deserted fort is a wonderful site if you are partial to ruined temples and forgotten, unvisited romantic monuments.

Kalanjar

This historical site is situated about 100 kms from Khajuraho and connected by motorable road. The fort is situated on an isolated flat-topped hill of the Vindhya range. It has an ancient history going back to the age of myths when the gods roamed the earth. In the middle of the 11th century it was captured by Shri Yashovarman, the seventh Chandella ruler.

Once you ascend the 240 metres, almost perpendicular hillside (a motorable road was built and if it has not been washed away by the monsoons, take it). Walking up one passes through several gateways built by the successive rulers who conquered and lived at Kalanjar. Within the fort there are palaces and remains of brick and stucco structures, and in addition two lovely reservoirs, Patal Ganga and Pandu Kund with the remains of the beautiful religious sculpture. The most intriguing spot is the Nilkantha Temple situated in a dark grotto on the western face of the Kalanjar plateau. Along the steps leading down to the temple are magnificent sculptures with inscriptions honouring the donors and patrons of Kalanjar. The temple has a carved, now ruined entrance *mandap* which leads into the natural cave. Within the cave is the ancient linga, the phallic image representing Shiva. From the base of the linga flows clear mountain water. The image is still in worship and thousands of devotees climb the steep mountainside on festive occasions.

Nacchna

It is about 100 kilometres from Khajuraho via Nagod. In a small temple complex there are two ancient temples belonging to the Gupta period (4 to 6th century AD). It is in these early temples that one can trace the growth and evolution of the central Indian style of architecture, which culminated in the splendid temples of Khajuraho. A special attraction of Nacchna is the exquisite and rare Shiva linga image. The linga, rather than being in the conventional symbolic phallic form, is carved with four heads held together by the central shaft. Each head, facing the cardinal directions, represents the faces of Shiva and the manifestations of the vital elements of life (Earth - East, the benign one; Fire - South, the fierce destroyer; Water - North the permanent one; Air - West, *nandin*, Space - Centre, the infinite).

Bandhavgarh National Park

This is one of the most beautiful national parks of Madhya Pradesh. The park is situated about 225 kilometres from Khajuraho in Shahdol district. Cars and buses are available on hire from Khajuraho to take you to Bandhavgarh National Park. The nearest railway station is Umaria and the distance is about 35 kilometres.

The best months to visit Bandhavgarh is between the months of November and March. It is suggested that you plan to spend two or three days to see the park. There is now a variety of accommodation to suit every budget: the **MP Tourism White Tiger Lodge** and the **Bandhavgarh Jungle Lodge**, while the **Bandhavgarh Jungle Camp** is set within the charming premises of the Maharaja's Hunting Lodge. The Bandhavgarh Jungle Camp has de luxe tented accommodation for 24 people. Park visits with a naturalist are also available.

The Bandhavgarh National Park covers an area of 437 square kilometres The park is dominated by the majestic Bandhavgarh fort built in the 14th century, with amazing early stone sculptures of the incarnations of Vishnu. There are historic caves in the fort and surrounding areas which have inscriptions that date back to the 2nd century BC to the 2nd Century AD.

There are many species of animals, birds and insects and plant life to be found in the park. Organized elephant or jeep rides through the many different areas of the park enable you to see animals in their natural habitat. The spotted deer, the Indian gazelle or *chinkara*, *nilgai*, *sambar*, wild boar, the tiny barking deer are frequently sighted. The sloth bear, bison, tiger and leopard are much more shy and correspondingly a rarer sight. There are a variety of eagles (including the regal serpent eagle), water fowl and storks, ibis, rare hornbills and the colourful golden-backed woodpecker. The park has beautiful grasslands and groves of bamboo.

HOW TO PLAN YOUR VISIT

In Khajuraho

Western Group of Temples	At least two hours
Eastern Group of Temples	At least one hour
Chaturbhuj Temple	Half an hour (sunset)
Site Museum	Half an hour

Arriving from Jhansi

Day 1 Datia, Orccha
Day 2 Orccha, Khajuraho
Day 3 Khajuraho
Day 4 In and around Khajuraho (Rajgrah Palace, Ken River, Panna National Park, Pandav Falls)
Day 5/6/7 Bandhavgarh National Park
From Bandhavgarh it is a seven-hour drive to Kanha National Park.

Or

Day 1 Jhansi, Orccha, Khajuraho
Day 2 Khajuraho
Day 3 In and around Khajuraho, Jhansi.
From Jhansi it is possible to visit other historic sites: Orccha, Datia, Shivpuri, Deogarh and Chanderi.

Arriving from Agra (by Plane)

Day 1 Khajuraho
Day 2 In and around Khajuraho
(2 - 3 days at Bandhavgarh National Park)
Day 3 Varanasi.

Excursion Routes from Khajuraho

Ajaygarh Fort—80 kilometres.
Bandhavgarh National Park—225 km.
Benisagar Lake—11 kilometres.
Dhubela Museum—64 kilometres.
Gangau Dam—34 kilometres.
Jhansi (Datia, Orccha)—175 km.
Kalanjar Fort—100 kilometres.

Majhgawan—56 kilometres.
Nacchna—100 kilometres.
Pandav Waterfalls—30 kilometres.
Panna National Park—48 kilometres.
Rajgarh Palace—25 kilometres.
Raneh Waterfalls—20 kilometres.
Ranguan Lake—25 kilometres.

FACTS FOR THE TRAVELLER

International Travel

A wide range of international flights from North America, Europe, West Asia, Southeast Asia and the Far East are available to Bombay, Calcutta and Delhi. Bombay also has flight connections with Africa.

Visas

Tourists are required to have a valid passport and most nationals require visas to enter India. If spending a long time in the region and planning to visit more than one country, a multiple-entry visa is advisable and best sought when making the original application.

Time Zones

Indian Standard Time follows 82° E longitude. IST is 5.5 hours ahead of GMT, 10.5 hours ahead of American Eastern Standard Time (New York), 4.5 hours behind Australian Eastern Standard Time and 3 hours behind Japanese Standard Time (Tokyo).

Internal Travel

Both national and private airlines provide a good network of flights of reasonable frequency within India. **Indian Airlines** prides itself on being the second largest domestic airline in the world, and its services have recently been augmented by new, privately-owned, internal airlines.

Airline security is generally strict and thorough. What can be taken on board as hand luggage often varies with international convention. Batteries of any type are not allowed: they are often removed from cameras. In some airports the local police security disallow lap-top computers, tape-recorders, radios, and pocket knives. All hand baggage is X-rayed, but most airports allow film to be inspected by hand. Some airports, such as Bombay, Colombo, Karachi, and Delhi also X-ray checked-in baggage.

The **rail network** in the subcontinent makes this one of the most convenient, economical and enjoyable ways of travelling within India. One of the exhilarating experiences of travel in the region is a journey on the Indian Railways. The vast network and frequency of trains makes rail travel not only pleasurable (I hope) but in many cases most suitable for reaching some of the more remote sites in the country.

Roads are the most direct way of reaching places in India. All areas have bus services of varying standards of comfort and efficiency. In many cases this is the only way of reaching a site by public transport. For long distances a combination of train and bus travel is the most economical and convenient. Long bus journeys are generally uncomfortable. On many long routes 'video coaches' operate, subjecting all the passengers to the conductors' favourite film. Some state transport corporations and tourist organizations operate air-conditioned buses on trunk routes and stop every two to three hours at roadside restaurants. It is advisable to book in advance for longer journeys. A few travel companies and hotels organize round-trip excursions by coach to nearby towns and sites. Many hotels and private agencies operate same day return trips.

Car rental in the region takes two forms. The facility to hire self-driven cars is fairly recent and is limited to major cities. Hiring a car with driver is not only cheaper but generally more convenient as the driver often doubles as guide, and this is possible in almost any town; although the standards of maintenance of the car in some of the smaller ones might raise a few questions or eyebrows.

Within a city travel by taxi (black with bright yellow hoods) and auto-rickshaws is often more economical. Insist on the use of the meter or come to an agreement on the rate before you set off. Cycle-rickshaws and *tongas* (horse-pulled carts) are available in most places, and are a fun way of covering short distances.

Inland Travel Concessions

Foreign tourists and non-resident Indians are offered several package deals, concessional fares and travel schemes for both air and rail travel.

Indian Airlines offers a 21-days '**Discover India**' trip for US$ 400. This allows for 21 days of unlimited travel on domestic flights. Those in the age group 12 to 30 years can avail of the **Youth Fare Concession** which amounts to 75 per cent of the fare on all domestic sectors of Indian Airlines for 120 days of unlimited travel. All payments have to be made in foreign exchange.

Indian Railways, the fourth-largest rail network in the world, offers an 'Indrail Pass' facility to foreign nationals and non-resident Indians The tickets may be purchased for a specific class of accommodation, and provides unlimited travel for a period of 7/15/21/30/60/90 days on any train which has that class of accommodation.

Security

While extremely wealthy in its cultural heritage, there are many poor people in the subcontinent: be kind to them and don't flash your wealth or patronize them. Begging should not be encouraged. Travel in India is, happily, still remarkably safe. Money, passports, tickets and valuables should be kept on one's person all the time. Don't leave items that might invite attention lying unlocked in hotel bedrooms or public places. Travelling by train or bus demands special alertness.

A few special precautions are advisable. It is best, for instance, to avoid those areas in the subcontinent that are facing political difficulties.

Currency

The India monetary unit is the rupee, consisting of 100 paise. Indian coins come in denominations of 5, 10, 20, 25 and 50 paise and 1, 2 and 5 rupees. Currency notes are in denominations of 1, 2, 5, 10, 20, 50, 100 and 500.

When this book went to press US$1 was approximately Rs 30/- and UK £1, approximately Rs 47/-.

Electricity

220 volt AC single phase is the standard domestic supply in India. But voltage tends to fluctuate, especially during the summer power shortages.

Health

Everything thrives in the tropics so take a few simple precautions to safeguard your health when travelling in the subcontinent.

Yellow fever certificates are required for all travellers arriving from Africa, Latin America and Papua New Guinea. Other vaccinations, although not officially required, are advisable. Typhoid, polio, and tetanus are important but a meningitis vaccine is required only when visiting infected areas, information about which will be available with local travel clinics. Infectious hepatitis can largely be avoided by taking a gamma globulin injection just before leaving for the subcontinent. While cholera is endemic and there are occasional outbreaks in the region, immunization is not mandatory. An anti-rabies vaccine is now available and advisable if travelling off the beaten track. A booster or fresh course of injections is necessary if bitten by a dog or any wild animal.

Malaria is widespread throughout the region. Opinion on what pills to take is constantly being revised: advice from a local travel clinic must be sought before starting a journey. It is important to begin the course before arriving and continue it for at least six weeks after leaving an infected area.

Most modern medicines are available over the counter in drugstores but it is wise to travel with reserve stock. If any prescription drugs are required, bring enough for the duration of the trip. It is sometimes best

Visitors at Lakshman Temple entrance

to keep two stocks of medicine: one in hand baggage and the other in checked-in baggage.

A small health kit should include a remedy for upset stomachs, some antiseptic cream, lip salve, mosquito-repellant cream, suntan lotion, water-purifying tablets in case bottled water is not available, antiseptic lotion, Elastoplast, etc. Many travellers develop minor problems on their second or third day as a result of 'climate shock' due to heat exhaustion rather than contaminated food and water, but if an upset stomach persists seek medical advice. Many people advise drinking a lot of fluids (boiled and filtered water with a little salt and sugar) and keeping to a diet of rice and yoghurt for a couple of days.

The standard advice is to drink only bottled or mineral water, avoid peeled fruit, and fresh salads and, despite the delicious cuisine of the subcontinent, go easy for the first few days.

Hotel Bills

All foreigners, except those specially exempted, are required to settle their

Shopping Centre, in front of Western Group of Temples, Khajuraho

hotel bills directly in foreign exchange. Credit cards are widely accepted in all major towns and hotels.

Tipping

Tipping is expected for most hotel and restaurant services in India. About 10 per cent of the bill is a reasonable tip. In many of the large cities, the big tourist hotels include a service charge in their bills, but an additional tip is generally expected.

Languages

Hindi is the national language but is, generally speaking, only the *lingua franca* of north India. Each state speaks in its own regional language, of which there are many dialects as well. But English will get you around most urban and tourist centres in India.

Media

India has a number of English-language daily newspapers and magazines catering to varied interests and tastes. *The Times of India*, *The Hindustan Times* and *The Statesman* are the leading newspapers in the north, and *The Hindu* is the leading daily in the south. The South-based *Indian Express*, however, is the only paper that publishes in all parts of the country except in the east. *India Today* is the leading news magazine. International editions of *Time* and *Newsweek* are available in news stands in all major cities.

India also has a wide network of radio and television stations. With the introduction of satellite television, news and programmes from around the world is also available.

Numbers and Measurements

India has now fully adopted the metric system; weights, distances and volume are measured in grams, kilograms, metres, kilometres and litres. But it is not uncommon for 'mile' or 'feet' or 'pound' to slip into the conversation: old habits die hard.

Temperature in India is officially measured in centigrade, but is spoken of in both measures. (100°C = 212°F; 0°C = 32°F).

Indians talk of large numbers in terms of lakhs and crores. A lakh is one hundred thousand and is written 1,00,000, while a crore is 10 million or 100 lakhs and is written 1,00,00,000.

Communications

Most towns have direct-dial facilities for both local and international calls. Many markets have privately run public call booths which are extremely reasonable. Most hotels mark up their communication tariffs by 100 per cent (if not more), so check the rates before use. Almost all hotels now have telex and fax facilities.

Photography

India is a photographer's paradise.

Taking photographs of airports, railway stations, bridges, military installations and from the air is prohibited in India. You can freely photograph all the monuments mentioned in this book with a hand-held camera. Permission is, however, required to take photographs in museums.

Special permission for professional photography (with tripod and flash), movie camera, or video is obtained from The Archaeological Survey of India (alongside the National Museum, Janpath, New Delhi). Permission cannot generally be given at the site. When taking photographs of people use the standard 'do unto others what you do not mind being done to yourself/your wife/family'.

Colour print film is now readily available in all major cities of the region but the price and vintage varies. Most hotel shops are more expensive than the nearby market. Only a limited range of slide film is generally available and Kodachrome only rarely. Bring a good supply of film: some photographers suggest at least twice the amount you expect to use. If travelling in summer keep film cool. It is best to develop film at home, rather than in India, to ensure best results. Film left over at the end of a trip makes a welcome present for someone who has been of assistance.

Working Hours and Holidays

Sunday is the weekly holiday. Many offices are closed on Saturdays or
work half a day. All government offices are closed on Saturdays and Sundays.
Other than these, the Indian calendar is replete with festival holidays, but
these tend to vary from state to state. There are three national holidays:
January 26—Republic Day, 15 August—Independence Day and 2 October—
Mahatma Gandhi's Birthday.

Office hours are generally 10 am to 5 pm, though they may vary with
the nature of the work and from state to state. Government offices work
from 9.30 am to 5.30 pm. Shops are open from 9 am to 7 pm, with
a lunch break from 1 pm to 3 pm. Smaller shops and pavement traders
keep flexible hours.

Bathing at Shiv Sagar, Khajuraho

Information
About
Khajuraho

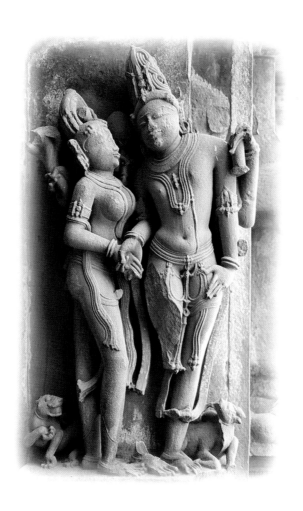

INFORMATION ABOUT KHAJURAHO

Khajuraho is a small village in central India. From the village one can see outcrops of the Vindhyan range. The Ken river that meanders along the outskirts of Khajuraho flows northwards to meet the Ganga river.

Location

The village of Khajuraho is located in Chattarpur district of Madhya Pradesh State.
Latitude: 24° 51, North Longitude: 79° 56, East
Altitude: 457 metres
The village of Khajuraho, with the expansion of the tourist industry, is growing every year. The total area of the village is approximately 21 square kilometres.

Climate

Khajuraho is located in central India, far from the sea breezes of the coastlands and the cool climes of the Himalaya.

Temperature Chart

Season	Maximum		Minimum	
	Celsius	Fahrenheit	Celsius	Fahrenheit
Summer (April – Sept)	47°	117°	21°	70°
Winter (Sept – March)	32°	90°	4°	40°
Rainfall (Annual)	1120 mm Monsoon Jul - Aug			

When to go

The best time to visit Khajuraho is during the months of October to March when the average temperature is between 90° and 40° fahrenheit.

What to wear

From October to March the days are warm and the nights cool. Khajuraho is familiar with tourists from every country and their styles and fashions. Loose, light clothing, cotton shirts and trousers is the most appropriate when visiting the temples.

Footwear should be light and easy as you are required to remove shoes on entry into the temples. Removal of shoes is customary in all sacred Hindu temples for purposes of cleanliness and also helps to protect the ancient monuments.

How to get there

Khajuraho is well-connected by air and road.

by Air

Khajuraho has an airport that is linked with daily services from Delhi, Agra and Varanasi by Indian Airlines and ModiLuft.

Flight time
>   Delhi to Agra: 35 minutes approx.
>   Agra to Khajuraho: 40 minutes approx.
>   Varanasi to Khajuraho: 45 minutes approx.

Flight information
>   **Indian Airlines Office**
>   Hotel Clarks Bundela, Khajuraho Tel 2035

>   Kanchenjunga Building,
>   Barakhamba Road, New Delhi Tel 3313732

>   **ModiLuft**
>   Hotel Clarks Bundela, Khajuraho Tel 2060

>   Khajuraho Airport: Tel 2036

by Train

There is no direct rail connection to Khajuraho. The most convenient station is Jhansi which is linked to Delhi and other major northern cities. The Superfast Shatabdi Express train from Delhi to Jhansi takes four hours approximately. From Jhansi Railway Station a number of buses and taxis ply to Khajuraho. The journey of 175 kilometres takes approximately four hours. Satna is on the Bombay to Allahabad line of the Central Railways and is a convenient railhead from Delhi, Bombay, Calcutta and Varanasi. From Satna Station taxis ply to Khajuraho, 117 kilometres away. Another nearby railway station is Harpalpur on the Jhansi to Manikpur line of the Central Railways. The distance of Khajuraho from Harpalpur is 100 kilometres.

by Road

Direct buses are available from Jhansi, Satna, Harpalpur, Agra, Gwalior, Bhopal, Indore, Chattarpur, Jabalpur.

From Jhansi to Khajuraho

The Madhya Pradesh Tourism A/C coach awaits the arrival of the Shatabdi Express train to ply passengers to Khajuraho. The journey of 175 kilometres takes approximately fours hours.

The fare on the M.P.Tourism A/C coach is Rs 150 per adult, Rs 80 per child (3 to 12 years).

There are other buses plying on this route. From Jhansi Railway Station ordinary buses take about five to six hours.

From Satna to Khajuraho

From the Satna Railway Station the bus stand is about 1 kilometres. The distance to Khajuraho from Satna is about 117 kilometres and takes about three hours.

From Mahoba to Khajuraho

Distance is about 65 kilometres and the journey time about two hours.

Distance of Some Important Places From Khajuraho

Agra	395 kilometres.	Jhansi	175 kilometres.
Allahabad	285 kilometres.	Lucknow	287 kilometres.
Bhopal	372 kilometres.	Mahoba	65 kilometres.
Bombay	1251 kilometres.	Panna	44 kilometres.
Chattarpur	50 kilometres.	Rewa	167 kilometres.
Delhi	598 kilometres.	Satna	117 kilometres.
Gwalior	276 kilometres.	Varanasi	415 kilometres.
Jabalpur	296 kilometres.		

Bandhavgarh Jungle Camp

People

There are approximately 6,000 inhabitants of Khajuraho, but the number is growing with the development of hotels and the tourist industry.

Religion: The village of Khajuraho is peopled primarily by Hindus,with a small community of Jains, Muslims and others.

Languages spoken: Khajuraho belongs to the historical Bundelkhand region and has its own very lyrical Bundelkhandi dialect. Hindi and English are now spoken by most inhabitants.

The Tourist Guides can speak several languages, including English French, Spanish, Italian, Japanese, German.

Where to Stay

Accommodation at Khajuraho ranges from well-managed five star luxury hotels to friendly guest-houses and budget hotels. (Tariffs given are subject to change).

Luxury Hotels

Hotel Chandella
On the Airport Road
District Chattarpur, Khajuraho 471606, Madhya Pradesh.

Management: Taj Group of Hotels
Tel: (076861) 2054, 2101 - 10
Fax: (076861) - 2095

Five Star A/C. No. of Rooms: 102
Tariff Single: $ 38; Double: $ 68.
There are also Executive and Deluxe suites.
All rooms are air-conditioned, have telephones, attached baths with hot and cold running water, showers, colour TV with in-house movies and satellite television. The hotel is located in a landscaped 11-acre garden with an inviting swimming pool. Other facilities: 24-hour room service, laundry, health club, beauty palour, restaurants and bars, bank and post office, car rental, doctor on call, shopping arcade for souvenirs and books. There are facilities for banquets and conventions.

Children of Khajuraho

Hotel Jass Oberoi
Near Chandella Hotel.
By-pass road, Khajuraho 471606, Madhya Pradesh
Management: Oberoi Group
Tel: (076861) - 2066, 2085 - 9
Fax: (076861) - 2088

Five Star A/C. No. of Rooms: 92
Tariff Single: $38; Double: $75
There are deluxe suites as well.
This is a well run hotel with all the facilities and comforts associated with luxury travel. All rooms have telephones, colour TV with in-house movies. The hotel has a health club, tennis courts, swimming pool, restaurant, bar, bank and post office, shopping arcade for travel agency, doctor-on-call, shops for souvenirs and books.

Two New Hotels in Khajuraho:

Holiday Inn
Airport Road, Khajuraho,
Tel: (076861) 2178
No. of Rooms: 56
Tariff Single: $ 38, Double: $ 70

Hotel Clarks Bundela
Airport Road, Khajuraho - 471606
Tel: (076861) 2363, 2365, 2360, 2366
Fax: (076861) 2359
Tariff Single: Rs 1,195, Double: Rs 2,250

Medium-priced Hotels

Hotel Khajuraho Ashok
On the Khajuraho - Rajnagar Road
Opposite the Circuit House
Khajuraho 471606, Madhya Pradesh

Management: Indian Tourism Development Corporation of India.
Tel: (076861) 2024
Fax: (076861) 2042

Three Star A/C. No. of Rooms: 38
Tariff Single: Rs 1,195; Double: Rs 1,400 (plus 10 per cent Luxury Tax).
All the rooms have attached baths, with hot and cold running water,
telephones and closed-circuit colour TV. Other facilities in the hotel are:
bank, laundry, swimming pool, restaurant and bar, and a shopping arcade.

The **Madhya Pradesh State Tourism Development Corporation** has a
number of reasonably priced, pleasant hotels in Khajuraho. Reservations
must be made more than five days in advance at:
Central Reservations, Tours Division MP State Tourism Development
Corporation Ltd., 4th floor, Gangotri, TT Nagar, Bhopal 462003
Tel: (0755) 554340 - 43

MP State Tourism Development Corporation Ltd.,
204 - 205, 2nd floor, Kanishka Shopping Plaza,
19, Ashoka Road, New Delhi 110001
Tel: (011) 3321187, 3324511

MP State Tourism Development Corporation Ltd.,
Tourist Bungalow Complex, Khajuraho 471606
Tel: (076861) 2051, 2221

Hotel Payal
> Management: Madhya Pradesh State Tourism
> Development Corporation (MPSTDC)
> Tel: (076861) 2076

No. of Rooms: 25 (14 ˙A/C, 11 Non A/C)
Tariff: Single A/C: Rs 400; Double A/C: Rs 450
Tariff Single Non A/C: Rs 200; Double Non A/C: Rs 250
Restaurant attached.

Hotel Jhankar
> Management: MPSTDC
> Tel: (076861) 2063

No. of rooms: 19
Tariff for Single A/C: Rs 400; Double A/C: Rs 450;
Single Non A/C: Rs 200; Double Non A/C: Rs 250
Facilities: Restaurant and bar.

Hotel Rahil
   Management: MPSTDC
   Tel : (076861) 2062

Non A/C No. of Double Rooms: 12
Dormitories: 72 beds
Tariff for Single Non A/C: Rs 130; Double Non A/C: Rs 150
Tariff for Dormitories: Rs 30 per head
Meals are available in the restaurant.

Tourist Bungalow
   Management: MPSTDC
   Tel: (076861) 2064

Non A/C No. of Rooms: 6
Tariff for Single Non A/C: Rs 175; Double Non A/C: Rs 225
No Dormitory.

Tourist Village Complex
   Management: MPSTDC
   Tel: (076861) 2128

Non A/C No. of Rooms: 13
Tariff for Single Non A/C: Rs 110; Double Non A/C: Rs 150
No Dormitories. Has a range of small charming cottages with attached
baths set in a garden. Also has a restaurant.

Circuit House
   Reservations with Collector
   Chattarpur/SDM, Rajnagar
   Tel: 2025
Non A/C and A/C.
Reserved for government officers and not open for visitors.

Budget Hotels

Jain Dharamshala
   For Jains only. Double rooms: 6; general rooms: 15; hall - 1
   Tariff double room and bath: Rs 150
   Tariff nominal: Rs 3 per person for group of 50

There are other small hotels, guest-houses and homes that offer reasonable
Indian style accommodation. Tariffs change with the tourist season:
approximately Rs 150 for a double room.

MOHAMMAD BILAL
KHAJURHO BICYCLE SHOP
ALQUILER DE LAS MEJORES BICICLETAS
NOLEGGIO BICICLETTE
BICYCLETTES A LOUER
FAHRRÄDER ZU VERMIETEN
FIETSEN TE HUUR
CYKELUTHYRNING

Important Khajuraho Telephone Numbers

Khajuraho STD Code Number   076861

Airport Office		2041
Archaeological Survey Site Museum		2032
Archaeological Survey of India		2039
Canara Bank		2071
Circuit House		2025
Government of India Tourist Office		2047
	Manager's Residence	2048
Hotels		
	Ashok	2024
	Chandella	2054
	Clarks Bundela	2363
	Harmony	2135
	Holiday Inn	2178
	Jass Oberoi	2085
	Natraj	2164
	Payal	2076
	Rahil	2062
	Surya Lodge	2145
	Tourist Bungalow	2064
	Tourist Village	2128
Indian Airlines		
	Station Manager	2035
	Airport	2036
Khajuraho Tours		2033
ModiLuft Airlines		2060
MPSTC Bus Stand		2090
MPSTDC Regional Office		2051
	Manager's Residence	2053
Police Station		
	Khajuraho	2032
	Rajnagar	2031
	Bamitha	2038
Post - Telegraph Office		2022
Telecom Bureau		2179
Tourist Information Counter Airport		2064
Travel Bureau		2037
State Bank of India		2017

Where to Eat

Restaurants in Hotels

Tend to be far more expensive. The coffee shops and restaurants at the Chandella and Jass Oberoi Hotel serve an assortment of Western and Indian food in air-conditioned comfort. The food at the MPSTDC run hotels tends to be far more satisfying with reasonably priced, less pretentious Indian food. Many new restaurants are mushrooming in and around Khajuraho village every year.

There are more than 15 eating houses in the quadrangle in front of the Western Group.

Raja Cafe

This is the most popular restaurant in Khajuraho. Raja Cafe was one of the first restaurants to be established in 1978. It is located across the road from the Western Group (opposite the Vishvanath Temple) and beside the Government of India Tourist Information office. The cafe sign claims that it is run by Swiss management. Western, Chinese and Indian cuisine is available. The most popular items on the menu are the Southern fried chicken and the chicken and mushroom pancake. It is a relaxing place to meet and chat between temple watching. Not expensive.

New Punjab Open Air Restaurant

Also opposite the Western Group of Temples. Serves North Indian Punjabi non-vegetarian and vegetarian food at moderate prices.

Madras Coffee Shop

It is situated across the road from the Western Group of Temples complex, on the southern side of the Memorial building. Specializes in South Indian cuisine: *dosa*, the rice flour pancake, *Idli*, rice flour dumplings, and other snacks. Good south Indian freshly ground coffee is usually available. Modest charges.

Lal Bungalow

Bijendra Singh, a well known guide, restored this historic 100 year old building, which was first a residence and then the old post office of Khajuraho. The building has now been converted into a charming restaurant. Specializes in Continental, Chinese and local vegetarian food. The **thali** or set-plate menu has an unlimited assortment of rice, *rotis*, vegetables, and *daal* at a reasonable price.

Drinking

Drinking alcohol in public places is prohibited by law in India. Most five star hotels in Khajuraho have bars and liquor licenses to serve customers and visitors.

There is a licensed liquor shop near Raja Cafe which sells Indian-made foreign liquor such as beer, vodka, gin and whiskey should you wish to drink in your hotel.

The prices are fixed and the shop opens according to government prescribed timings and is closed on all government holidays.

Lal Bungalow, once a post office now a restaurant

Banks and Money Changers

Please do not change foreign currency with helpful residents but use authorized banks.

State Bank of India
> Opposite Western Group of Temples. Tel: 2017.
> Timings: 10.45 to 2.45 pm and Saturday 10.45 to 12.45 pm.
> Closed on Sundays and other holidays.

Canara Bank
> Near Bus Stand, Shopping Centre. Tel: 2071
> Timings: 10 to 2 pm. Saturdays 10 to 12 pm. Sundays closed.
> Counter in Hotel Khajuraho Ashok. Timings: 10 am to 1.30 pm.

Post and Telegraph Offices

> Post Office, near Bus Stand. Tel: 2022
> Telecom Bureau, near Bus Stop. Tel: 2179

There are STD and international call booths on the Jain Temple Road and beside the entrance to the Western Group of Temples.

Meeting Place, Raja Cafe, Khajuraho

Tourist Information Counters

Govt. of India Tourist Information Centre
Opposite Western Group of Temples
Tel: 2047
Timings: 9 am to 17.30 pm. Saturdays and holidays 8 am to 12 am.
Closed on Sundays and national holidays.

Tourist Information Counter
Khajuraho Airport Tel: 2056
Open during flight hours only.

Information Centre
MP State Department of Tourism,
Tourist Bungalow
Tel: 2064

MPSTDC
Regional Manager, Khajuraho
Tel: 2051

For more details and information write to:

Director General
Archaeological Survey of India, Janpath, New Delhi 110001

Superintending Archaeologist
Archaeological Survey of India, Central Circle, Bhopal.

Director
MP State Tourism Development Corporation Ltd.
4th floor Gangotri, TT Nagar, Bhopal 462003 (MP)
Tel: 554340

The Curator
Archaeological Museum, Khajuraho
Tel: 2032

Regional Manager
Madhya Pradesh State Tourism Development Corporation Ltd.
Tourist Bungalow, Khajuraho (MP)
Tel: 2051

Hospital

There is a government hospital near the Khajuraho Bus Stand. Most hotels have a doctor on call. There is a chemist shop at the Khajuraho Bus Stand.

Entrance to the Temple Complex and Museum

The Western Group of Temples is open to visitors from sunrise to sunset each day. An entrance fee of Rs 0.50 admits you to the Western Group of Temples and the Archaeological Site Museum. Admission is free for children up to 15 years. Entrance to the Temple complex and Museum is free on Fridays.

The Archaeological Survey Museum opens daily from 9 am to 5 pm and is closed on Fridays.

Photography

Still photography is permissible without a fee. There is a charge of Rs 25 for use of a hand-held video camera, payment to be made at the entrance office at the Western Group of Temples. Photography with the use of a tripod, flash, video and movie camera of any of the temples at Khajuraho and the Archaeological Museum is permissible only with prior written permission from Director General, Archaeological Survey of India, Janpath, New Delhi 110001. No one in Khajuraho is authorized to sanction this permission.

Shopping

Khajuraho has no well known craft tradition. The village potter and basket-weaver supply local needs. A large number of shops selling clothes, souvenirs and 'antiques' have sprung up in the last few years.

There are a number of bookshops in Khajuraho that sell guides and picture books such as;

Classical Books near Raja Cafe and South Indian Crafts and Books in the row of shops beside the Jain Temple Complex.

Special Festivals at Khajuraho

February - March   **Maha-Shivarati** The great night of Shiva. Celebrated in Khajuraho as the wedding of Shiva and Parvati, it is attended by around 50,000 people from neighbouring villages. A village fair or *mela* is held, processions are taken out and prayers offered in the Matangeshvar Temple.

1st week of March   **Dance Festival** Every year a week-long dance festival is organized at Khajuraho. Eminent dancers perform the classical dance styles, Bharatnatyam, Kathak, Odissi and others, against the backdrop of the illuminated temples of the Western Group. Tickets are available at all major hotels and through travel agents in Khajuraho.

February – March   **Holi** The arrival of summer is celebrated across northern India. On the eve of Holi, bonfires of unwanted possessions symbolize the destruction of the demon Holika by the infant Krishna and also the death of winter and ushering in of spring rebirth. During Holi, social conventions are suspended until noon enabling men and women to flirt, shower each other with coloured powder and water, sing and dance in the streets.

March - April   **Mahavir Jayanti** Jains celebrate the birth of Mahavira, the 24th and last Tirthankara (teacher) who lived in the sixth century BC.

May - June	**Buddha Purnima** Buddhists celebrate the Buddha's birth, enlightenment and achievement of nirvana on one day, even though the events happened in different years.
August - September	**Janmashtami** This is Lord Krishna's birthday.
September - October	**Dussehra** A major all-India festival celebrating Lord Rama's victory over the demon Ravana who had captured his wife Sita.
October - November	**Diwali** A major Indian festival, known as the festival of lights, celebrating two events: Lord Rama's return home with Sita; the start of the Hindi financial new year (the official New Year is 13 April, a public holiday). Friends and relatives visit newly spring-cleaned homes bearing gifts of sweetmeats. There is much gambling; those who win will have Lakshmi's luck for the coming year. In the evening everyone lights tiny earthenware oil lamps (*diyas*) or candles in rows along the walls of gardens, roofs, doorways and balconies to show Rama and Sita the way home, as fireworks reverbrate and illuminate the earth and the sky.

Khajuraho Dance Festival

Guides

There are 26 licensed guides of the Department of Tourism in Khajuraho. Several of the guides speak a number of languages: English, French, Japanese, German, Spanish and Italian. In most cases their passion for exaggeration and desire to impress is greater than their knowledge and historical accuracy. They are a persuasive community and if your stay is short it may serve you well to hire a guide at least for the first day.

At present the Authorized Guide Fee is:
>   Half day: Rs 250 (1 - 4 pers.) Rs 400 (5 - 15 pers.)
>   Rs 500 (16 - 40 pers.)
>   Full day: Rs 350 (1 - 4 pers.) Rs 500 (5 - 15 pers.)
>   Rs 750 (16 - 40 pers.)

Guides can be contacted through the Tourist Office or at Raja Cafe. A full day s tour includes visits to the Western and Eastern Group of Temples, a break for lunch and some shopping.

Excursion Agents

There are several agents that can be contacted through your travel agency or hotel. These agents have A/C and Non A/C cars and A/C buses on hire. They can arrange excursions in and around Khajuraho for you.

Khajuraho Tours
>   BS Lawania
>   Opp. Western Group of Temples
>   Khajuraho (MP) 471606
>   Tel: 2033, 2123

Travel Bureau
>   Jain Mandir Road,
>   Khajuraho (MP) 471606
>   Tel: 2037, 2232

Has branches in Agra, Varanasi, Jhansi, Bhopal, Gwalior and other cities.

Tour Aids
Temple Hotel Complex
Khajuraho (MP) 471606

Pleasure Tours
Jain Mandir Road, Khajuraho
(MP) 471606

How to get Around

by Car

A/C and Non A/C cars and buses can be hired from the above agents. Rates for hire can be calculated as: local travel, outstation, night halt, airport transfer, half day sightseeing, full day sightseeing, half day sightseeing and one transfer, round trip to Raneh Waterfalls, Rajgarh Palace, Ken River Lodge, Panna National Park and other package excursions.

by Rickshaw

Cycle rickshaws can be hired from outside your hotel or the temple complex. The rates are not fixed and there are no meters. Bargain for the amount before you set off. The rickshaw can be hired for half a day, full day, or to visit specific groups of temples.

by Bicycle

Bicycles can be hired at a very reasonable rates—approximately Rs 10 for the entire day. This is a lovely way to travel around Khajuraho at your own pace.

on Foot

Distances within Khajuraho are not great. One can, if one has the time in the winter months, walk from the hotel to the Western and Eastern Group of Temples.

GLOSSARY

Architectural terms

amalaka stylised fruit associated with regeneration, incorporated at the summit of northern Indian *shikharas* as a support for the *kalash*.

antarala passage or vestibule leading to the sanctum of temple.

ashrama monastic retreat.

chakra wheel.

chhatri canopy or kiosk.

chowk court; courtyard; square.

darshan vision of divine grace; pilgrimage; homage.

darwaza (Persian) door, gate, or portal, especially of monumental proportions, usually prefixed with a name, e.g Dilli Darwaza meaning the Gate that leads to Delhi.

dharamsala the home of dharma; a monastic abode.

dhvaja standard, banner or flag; hence, *dhvaja stambha*, flag-staff.

dikpala regent of the cardinal directions of space; hence *ashta dikpalas*, regents of the eight directions of space.

durbar (Persian) royal assembly.

dvara door, hence *dvarapala*, door-keeper.

garbha-griha literally, 'womb chamber': inner sanctum of temple.

haveli mansion; merchant's house.

jali lattice or filigree-patterned screen.

kalash water pitcher, vase, used as a symbol of plenty; immortality.

kirtimukha literally 'Face of Glory': a grotesque mask; also called *grasamukha*, protector of worshipper from evil.

linga: the phallic symbol of Shiva; the mark of potential cosmic creativity; fertility.

mandap hall or pillared pavilion, of which the following are the most important types: *ardha-*(immediately before the sanctuary, when larger than an *antarala*); *maha-*(main).

markara mythical crocodile whose ever-watchful, wide-open eyes protect the building.

pradakshina patha circumambulatory path or passage around a shrine.

purna-kalash 'bowl of plenty'.

purnima full moon; auspicious night.

ratha temple chariot, sometimes used for shrine.

shastra traditional science; theoretical treatise.

shikhara northern temple superstructure; crowning cupola of southern temples.

stambha pillar; post, column.

surya sun: *surya mandir*, sun temple; *surya-vamsha*, descendants of the sun.

swayambhu self-existant; that was born of the self.

tirtha literally, 'fording place': place of spiritual regeneration; temple; hence, tirthankara, 'ford-maker'.

toran ceremonial portal, gateway.

vahan(a) vehicle or mount of god.

vajra thunderbolt; in Buddhist lore it is symbolic of power, hence, *vajrasana*, seat of the thunderbolt; *vajrapani*, the *bodhisattva* who holds the thunderbolt.

vastu residence, hence *vastushastra*, traditional science of architecture and *vastu-purush-mandala*, diagram for the residence of the Purusha; the formula for sacred building.

vyala lion; leopard; mythical guardian animals depicted in temple precincts.

Iconography

Abhaya Hand gesture of protection.

Agni Lord of Fire. Depicted in human form surrounded by flames, or just as a flame worshipped as part of all major Hindu rituals, as the purifier of the world, keeper of the hearth, etc. One of the principal deities in Vedic literature.

Ananta The infinite. A term applied to **Vishnu** and others.

Apsaras Celestial nymphs, seen flying above the gods, showering flowers, carrying umbrellas, garlands, etc.

Ardhanareshvar *See* **Shiva**.

Avatars of Vishnu *See* **Vishnu**.

Bhairava *See* **Shiva**.

Bhumidevi Bhumi, personification of the Earth goddess. *See* **Vishnu**; *also* Bhudevi, wife of Vishnu.

Bodhisattva Potential Buddha, renouncing nirvana to remain on earth for the benefit of humanity, to show others the middle path.

Chamunda *See* **Devi**.

Chand The personification of the moon.

Churning of the Ocean Often depicted in painting and sculpture, this refers to an episode at the beginning of time when the ocean was churned (like milk); ambrosia and all goodness appeared and the gods and demons fought to attain such powers. *See* **Kurma Avatar** under **Vishnu**.

Dakshinamurthi *See* **Shiva**.

Devi A general term for the female principle, female goddess (Sakti, the power). It is in the union of male and female, of two opposites, that the holistic concept of Hindu philosophy is to be understood.

Devi stands on a lotus pedestal, carrying a lotus in one hand. In her benign and terrifying form she may have a number of arms relaying her various attributes.

Durga The inaccessible one.

Kali Bhadrakali and Mahakali are the forms that the Devi assumes to destroy evil. Her form, with many arms, weapons of war and her terrifying expression frightens away her opponents (evil-doing enemies) and also destroys the fear of her devotees.

Mahishasuramardini Devi is created with all the powers of the gods to slay the demon buffalo Mahisha. She is often shown with several arms, beheading Mahisha who transforms himself from a buffalo into the form of a man but is eventually killed.

Uma/Parvati Shiva's wife, carrying a lotus in one hand, is often depicted seated or standing by Shiva's side.

Ekadanta *See* **Ganesh**.

Ganesh Ganapati, Vighnesvara or Vinayaka, the remover of obstacles and son of **Shiva** and **Parvati**.

Birth of Ganesh Parvati created Ganesh from dirt off her body. He served as her guard. On one occasion Shiva attempted to enter Parvati's bathing area and was stopped by Ganesh. Unknowingly, Shiva cut off the head of his son. Parvati, in her fury, demanded the return of her son's life, and Shiva replaced Ganesh's head with an elephant's head obtained from a herd nearby.

Ganesh has two wives, Buddhi and Siddhi, personification of wisdom and attainment of desire, respectively.

Ganapati One of his names as Lord of the *ganas*, or chief of the army of the gods. He is also said to have aided Vyasa in the composition of the Mahabharata.

Ekadanta Refers to Ganesh's elephant head being represented in iconography with one broken tusk.

Ek is one, the only supreme being; *danta*—tusk or tooth—is a symbol of strength and power. Hence Ekadanta is the all-powerful one. As one of India's most popular deities, he is worshipped at the commencement of every activity or venture.

There is a story that the moon (Chand) looked down at the elephant-headed baby and started to laugh. Ganesh snapped his tusk and hurled it at the moon who began to lose his brightness. Ganesh stopped the process, but the curse had been given and forevermore the moon will wax and wane

Ganesh is shown standing, sitting, and dancing. Due to his now rotund belly, he is rarely depicted in yogic posture but on a seat or throne. Ganesh's trunk turns towards the left (very rarely to the right). Apart from jewellery, Ganesh, like his father Shiva, wears a snake tied as a belt around his waist or across his chest, like the holy thread worn by caste Hindus. Ganesh has as his companion vehicle, or *vahana*, a rat that aids him in finding a way past all obstacles.

Ganga Personification of the goddess of the sacred river Ganga. The saint Bhagiratha prayed for her presence on earth to wash away the sins and ashes of the dead. Ganga descended with all her force, and Shiva took the weight of the mighty river on his head, the waters were lost in his curls, subdued by his presence. The river flows from the central Himalaya, through the northern plains of India, to the east where it meets the Bay of Bengal.

Garuda Mythical bird, the companion *vahana* (vehicle) of **Vishnu**, shown carrying his Lord or with human arms folded in prayer.

Hanuman Monkey chief, the faithful companion and devotee of **Rama** in the Ramayana.

white cloud. This Vedic deity was superseded by **Krishna** and others in later periods.

Jain From the term *jina*, meaning the victor, comes the term Jaina or Jain, meaning followers or sons of the victor.

Mahavir Jain was, like the Buddha, born of a princely family. He left home and took to a life of severe asceticism. His teachings revolve around the notion of life as a continuous struggle against desires. He spread the message of peace and *ahimsa* (non-violence) as the path of deliverance from the cycle of life.

Kali *See* **Devi.**

Kalki Avatar of Vishnu. *See* **Vishnu.**

Kalyanasundara *See* **Shiva.**

Karttikeya *See* **Skanda.**

Krishna Avatar of Vishnu *See* **Vishnu.**

Kurma Avatara *See* **Vishnu.**

Lakshmi The goddess of wealth emerging from the ocean and bathed by two elephants (Gajalakshmi). She represents all goodness. Lakshmi appears in all Vishnu's incarnations as Sita, wife of Rama, as Rukmini, Satyabhama, and Radha beside Krishna, etc. She carries lotuses, a pot of ambrosia and other emblems.

Linga Phallic symbol of Shiva. *See* **Shiva.**

Mahabharata Epic poem about the fortunes of the Pandava family.

Mahishasuramardini *See* **Devi.**

Matsya Avatar *See* **Vishnu.**

Naga, Nagadeva A race of sacred serpents who rule the underworld. They represent the water, the earth, and all the treasures derived from the earth. As snakes are crucial to farmers in loosening the soil and destroying rats who eat the grain, snake worship is common in almost all parts of India. They are portrayed alone, often with hoods and jewellery or entwined as couples (*naga* and *nagini*), and along with other deities like Shiva, Ganesh, etc.

Often seen with human heads and arms and snake-like bodies, they are said to be immortal, having tasted the ambrosia from the Churning of the Ocean (*see above*). They bring prosperity, marriage, and offspring to their devotees.

Nandi Bull. Companion (*vahana*, or vehicle) of Shiva.

Narasimha Avatar of Vishnu. *See* **Vishnu.**

Nataraja *See* **Shiva.**

Parasurama Avatar of Vishnu. *See* **Vishnu**.

Pashupati Shiva, lord of all creatures. *See* **Shiva**.

Rama Avatar of Vishnu. *See* **Vishnu**.

Ravana King of Lanka, who kidnapped Sita and was defeated by Rama in the Ramayana. Depicted with ten heads, he is described in literature as a brave and well-read man. Unfortunately, his weakness (lust) was the cause of his downfall.

Saraswati Goddess of learning and of all knowledge and wisdom. Her symbols are a book (palm leaf), holy beads, a *vina* (stringed musical instrument), and the lotus. She is assigned to Brahma as his companion.

Sesha The serpent that floats on the sea of eternity. *See* **Anantasesha** under **Vishnu**.

Shiva A supreme deity, one of the trinity of Vishnu, Brahma, and Shiva, symbolizing preservation, creation, reabsorption, and re-creation (achieved sometimes through destruction).

MANIFESTATIONS OF SHIVA:

   (i)   Without form, the supreme being with no beginning and no end.

  (ii)   The luminous pillar or *linga* (phallic symbol), the emerging form that is limitless in its power.

        The pillar appears in a story from the Shiva Purana, when Vishnu and Brahma contest supremacy. Shiva turns into a never-ending luminous pillar, Brahma and Vishnu strive to find the end of the pillar and in failing to do so underline Shiva's supremacy.

        The *linga* rests on a *yoni* stone, symbolizing the female principle and is often rounded or faceted. In rare cases a face or many faces appear on its side, as in the Pashupati temple in Kathmandu.

 (iii)   The third is the human form that Shiva assumes for the benefit of his devotees.

        Shiva is described firstly as an ascetic wearing the skin of a tiger or a simple loincloth. Snakes twine around his wrist and neck, like jewels, for he is also lord of the underworld. In his hair Shiva wears the crescent moon as a jewel to symbolize this aspect as 'conqueror of time and all that changes'. He wears a *datura* flower in his matted sage-like hair. As in all depictions of deities, Shiva has many forms and many arms, limbs and heads to manifest his various attributes.

Shiva is described firstly as an ascetic wearing the skin of a tiger or a simple loincloth. Snakes twine around his wrist and neck. like jewels, for he is also lord of the underworld. In his hair Shiva wears the crescent moon as a jewel to symbolize this aspect as 'conqueror of time and all that changes'. He wears a *datura* flower in his matted sage-like hair. As in all depictions of deities, Shiva has many forms and many arms, limbs and heads to manifest his various attributes.

Ardhanareshvara A composite figure, half-man and half-woman, Shiva and *Parvati* united to symbolize the reconciliation of opposites to create a holistic entity. The male half wears a different headdress, clothing and jewellery. The female side curves gracefully, relaxed and in repose.

Bhairav 'The terrible' form of Shiva, with an awesome expression, as an ascetic with little clothing accompanied by a dog.

Dakshinamurti The ascetic and teacher, Shiva is seated in yogic posture, surrounded by animals and devotees.

Gangadhara Shiva is said to have borne the weight of the great river Ganga as it fell down onto the earth. Ganga is depicted as a female goddess often perched in Shiva's hair, much to the annoyance of *Parvati*, Shiva's jealous wife.

Hari Hara Composite image of Vishnu and Shiva.

Kalyanasundara Shiva as a handsome prince at the time of his marriage to *Parvati*.

Nataraja Shiva dancing the dance of creation. He often stands with one leg raised, the other trampling Apasmara, the symbol of ignorance. He is often depicted with four arms: one carries a flame (destruction), the second a *damru* (a little drum that beats out the rhythm of creation), the third hand in *abhaya mudra* (protection), and the fourth pointing to his foot (denoting salvation from ignorance). His hair spreads out in waves, and there is often a halo of fire around his swirling form.

Pashupati Lord of All Creatures. Shiva usually has his trident in one hand and a deer in the other.

Shiva - Parvati Seen often as husband and wife, seated with their two children, Ganesh and Karttikeya, and their animal companions (Nandi, Shiva's bull, Parvati's tiger, Ganesh's rat, and Karttikeya's Peacock).

Surya The lord of the sun rides across the sky on a chariot drawn by seven horses (the seven colours of the rainbow), usually carrying two lotuses in his hand. He wears high boots, and the armour covering his chest has given rise to a belief that his image is of foreign origin. He is accompanied by his charioteer, the lame Aruna. His female companions or handmaidens include Rajni, Usha, and Chhaya—radiance, dawn, and shade, respectively. Usha and Pratyusha drive away the darkness with their bows and arrows.

Tirthankara(s) There are ten regions of the universe, each with 24 Tirthankaras in each of the three ages—past, present, and future. They take the part of teachers who, by example, lead the way to salvation. Adhinath, Parshvanath, and Mahavir (*see* **Jaina**) were three of the Tirthankaras.

Tripurantaka *See* **Shiva**.

Trivikrama *See* **Vishnu**.

Uma *See* **Devi**.

Vajra Thunderbolt.

Vamana Avatar of Vishnu. *See* **Vishnu**.

Varaha Avatar of Vishnu. *See* **Vishnu**.

Venugopal Krishna, the flute player.

Vinayaka *See* **Ganesh**.

Vishapaharana *See* **Shiva**.

Vishnu In ancient lore Vishnu was one amongst the Vedic deities, but subsequently was elevated to form part of the trinity of Brahma, Shiva, and Vishnu.

Vishnu is shown in three positions, standing, sitting, and reclining. When he is standing with one hand raised in the *abhaya* hand gesture, he is offering protection to his devotees.

In one hand Vishnu carries the *shank*, or conch, used to blow the call to battle, the sound of salvation. In his other hand is the *chakra*, or disc, a circular wheel with spokes that is flung at the enemy, cutting off their heads and arms, the symbol of protection. He also carries the lotus of creation and a wooden club, the symbol of destruction. Vishnu's consorts are Lakshmi, who sits to his right, and Bhumidevi on the left. They are the attributes of wealth and the prosperity of the earth, and carry a lotus and a lily, respectively.

Anantasesha The image of Vishnu reclining on the serpent Sesha that floats on the sea of eternity. Lakshmi is seated beside Vishnu and Bhumidevi is often shown pressing his feet. The *vahana* of Vishnu is Garuda, identified with the Brahminy kite, a large, beautiful chestnut-coloured bird found in India.

In one hand Vishnu carries the *shank*, or conch, used to blow the call to battle, the sound of salvation. In his other hand is the *chakra*, or disc, a circular wheel with spokes that is flung at the enemy, cutting off their heads and arms, the symbol of protection. He also carries the lotus of creation and a wooden club, the symbol of destruction. Vishnu's consorts are Lakshmi, who sits to his right, and Bhumidevi on the left. They are the attributes of wealth and the prosperity of the earth, and carry a lotus and a lily, respectively.

Anantasesha The image of Vishnu reclining on the serpent Sesha that floats on the sea of eternity. Lakshmi is seated beside Vishnu and Bhumidevi is often shown pressing his feet. The *vahana* of Vishnu is Garuda, identified with the Brahminy kite, a large, beautiful chestnut-coloured bird found in India.

INCARNATIONS OR AVATARS OF VISHNU In every cycle of decadence Vishnu is said to come to earth to save her from destruction. Vishnu is seen sometimes surrounded by his ten avatars.

Matsya Avatar Vishnu appears in the form of a huge fish, or half-fish and half-man.

The legend tells of a sage who caught a small fish and put it in a bowl. The fish grew too big for the bowl and the lake, and had to be taken out to sea. This fish saved the universe that was overwhelmed by a deluge. The fish avatar is also said to have saved the Vedas and holy books from the floods.

Kurma Avatar Vishnu appears as a tortoise that served as a gigantic pedestal in the episode referred to as the Churning of the Ocean. The gods and demons churned the ocean at the beginning of time as one churns milk to make butter. By churning the ocean, good and evil rose to the surface, and ambrosia—the formula for eternal and youthful life—was brought forth from the waters. In order to churn the mighty ocean, the gods needed a churning rod. For this they used a mountain, and Vishnu, as a tortoise, provided the support to hold the rod in place.

Varaha Avatar From the deluge at the origin of the earth Vishnu, in the form of a giant boar, lifted up the earth (goddess) out of the waters of creation.

Vishnu's form is often shown as half-man with a face of a boar that has picked up the earth, *bhu*, personified as a little goddess (Bhuvaraha).

Narasimha Avatar Vishnu appears with a lion's head and human body, usually with the evil man Hiranyakasipu, who is being torn apart and devoured on his lap. The story relates that Hiranyakasipu obtained many boons from the gods and declared himself infallible. No one, neither man nor beast, could kill him, no weapon could injure him, neither by day nor by night, outside or within the house. Perturbed by his power, the gods requested Vishnu to destroy Hiranyakasipu. Vishnu assumed the form of half-man and half-lion, and at dusk, at the threshold of the house (neither inside nor outside), he tore the demon to pieces.

Vamana Avatara (Trivikrama) In sculpture and painting Vamana, or Vishnu, is usually depicted as a dwarf or small man who is receiving a gift from King Bali. In order to teach Bali a lesson Vamana asks for a gift of three paces of land. How much land can the dwarf take in three paces thinks Bali and agrees to make the gift. Vishnu steps out of the Vamana form and places one foot to conquer the earth, another that stretches from earth to heaven and looks for a third pace. Bali, realizing Vishnu's greatness, offers his head, acknowledging defeat. In sculpture Vishnu is shown stretching out his leg to take the three paces (*tri* meaning three plus *vikrama* meaning victory). The repentant Bali was then appointed lord of the underworld.

Parasurama Very rarely to be seen, Vishnu in human form holds a *parasu* (battleaxe) in one hand. Born a Brahmin, he took to the ways of a *kshatriya* (warrior) and slew his mother for her lustful ways.

Rama This avatar of Vishnu is the hero of the epic Ramayana and, with his wife Sita and brother Lakshmana, is widely so depicted in sculpture and painting. Rama usually holds a bow, Sita stands to his right, and Lakshmana, a little shorter than Rama, often carries a bow. Hanuman, the monkey lord, is often shown with this group.

Krishna Is usually depicted with the attributes of Vishnu: the conch and the disc. He wears a peacock-feather crown, a flaming yellow dhoti, garlands and flowers. His skin is said to be dark like the blue-black rain clouds, symbolic of his goodness.

His lover as a cowherd was Radha. Krishna's chief wives are Rukmini and Satyabhama. From childhood in Mathura and Brindavan (UP), Krishna went to live in Dwaraka (Gujarat).

Krishna reappears in the Mahabharata epic. He plays the charioteer and philosopher - guide to Arjun during the great battle to explain the

Bhagavat Gita (Song of the Divine One) which encapsulates the essence of Hindu philosophy.

Balkrishna Krishna as a child often depicted dancing with a butter ball, crawling about and playing.

Kaliyakrishna and Goverdhana Krishna's childhood as a cowherd is described in many scenes: with his mother Yasodha killing the demon horse, conquering the serpent Kaliya, breaking away from the cart and mortar, stealing butter, dancing with a butter ball, playing with the *gopis* and girls of the village, lifting up Mount Goverdhana to protect cows and humans from the storm sent by Lord Indra.

Venugopal An avatar of Vishnu as the boy cowherd, Venugopal—Krishna as the player of the *venu* (flute)—plays music, luring his followers, the cowherds and cows.

In order to free the world from oppression, Krishna was born to kill the wicked King Kamsa. The king had imprisoned Devaki, prophesied to be the holy mother. Her child was smuggled out at birth and given to Yasodha to look after. This scene is depicted as a stormy night, with a child being carried away in a basket. King Kamsa is dashing a child to the ground, in an attempt to kill all infants he thinks might destroy him.

Buddha Also considered to be an avatar of Vishnu (incorporated in the medieval period).

Kalki The avatar of Vishnu that is yet to come, at the end of this *kaliyuga* (time cycle) when the world dissolves into decadence. Virtue and justice disappear, then Kalki (horse and rider) will come and free the world of evil.

Yaksha/Yakshi Celestial, supernatural beings, associated with wealth and prosperity. Usually female forms holding flowers or branches of trees that blossom at their touch.

Yamuna The river is personified as a goddess riding on a tortoise carrying a pot of her holy waters.

Yashodha Krishna's mother. *See* **Krishna** under **Vishnu**.

yogi one who practices the discipline of *yoga*; fem. **yogini**, also refers to manifestation of the great goddess.

FURTHER READING

Agrawal, U. *Khajuraho Sculptures and their significance.* Chand Co., Delhi, 1964.

Anand, Mulk Raj. *Homage to Khajuraho.* Marg Publications, Bombay, 1957.

Bose, N.S. *History of the Chandellas of Jejakabhukti.* Firma KLM, Calcutta, 1956.

Burt, T.S. *Journal of the Asiatic Society of Bengal.* Vol. VIII, Jan-Dec, 1839.

Chakravarty, Kalyan Kumar. *The Art of Khajuraho.* Arnold-Heinemann Publishers, New Delhi, 1985.

Cunningham, Alexander. *Archeological Survey of India Reports. A Tour of the Central Provinces.* Vol. IX, 1873-75.

Desai, Devangana. *Erotic Sculpture of India: A Socio-cultural Study.* Tata McGraw Hill Pub. Co., New Delhi, 1975.

Dhama, B.L. *A Guide to Khajuraho.* Times of India Press, Bombay, 1927.

Dikshit, R.K. *The Chandellas of Jejakabhukti.* Abhinav Publications, New Delhi, 1977.

Dowson, John. *A Classical Dictionary of Hindu Mythology and Religion.* Lyall Book Depot, Delhi.

Eck, Diana L. *Banaras City of Light.* Routledge & Kegan Paul, London, 1983.

Keay, John. *India Discovered.* Collins, London, 1988.

Krishna Deva. *Guide to Khajuraho Museum.* A.S.I., New Delhi, 1973.

Khajuraho, A.S.I., New Delhi, reprinted 1987.

Khajuraho, Brijbasi Printers Pvt. Ltd., New Delhi, 1987.

Temples of Khajuraho. A.S.I., New Delhi, 1990.

Lal, Kunwar. *Erotic Sculptures of Khajuraho.* Asia Publishers, Delhi, 1970.

Nath, Ram. *The Art of Khajuraho.* Abhinav Publications, New Delhi, 1980.

Poddar, Pramila. *Temples of Love: Khajuraho.* Luster Press, New Delhi, 1992.

Prakash, Vidya. *Khajuraho: A Study in the Cultural Conditions of Chandella Society.* Taraporevala Son & Co., Bombay, 1967.

Punja, Shobita. *Divine Ecstasy: Story of Khajuraho*. Viking, Penguin Books, New Delhi, 1992

Museums of India. The Guidebook Company Ltd., Hong Kong, 1990.

Great Monuments of India, Bhutan, Nepal, Pakistan and Sri Lanka. The Guidebook Company Ltd., Hong Kong, 1994.

Rai, Raghu. *Khajuraho*. Time Books International, New Delhi, 1990.

Spear, P. *A History of India*. Vol. II. Penguin, Harmondsworth, rpt. 1978.

Thapar, R. *A History of India*. Vol. I. Penguin, Harmondsworth, rpt. 1978.

Trivedi, R.D. *Temples of the Pratihara Period in Central India*. A.S.I., New Delhi, 1990.

Zannas, Eliky. *Khajuraho*. Intro by J. Auboyer. Mouton & Co., The Hague, 1960.

The Archeological Survey of India publishes an excellent (inexpensive) series of booklets on many of the major sites in India.

Guide to Khajuraho, A.S.I., New Delhi

Guide to Khajuraho Museum, A.S.I., New Delhi

The Guidebook Company Ltd., Hong Kong, Odyssey Guides Series:

Introduction to

India

Delhi, Agra & Jaipur;

Goa

The Museums of India

The Hill Stations of India

Birds of India

Our World in Colour Series:

Khajuraho, Banaras, Ajanta & Ellora, Delhi, Agra & Jaipur, Garhwal and Kumaon, Goa, Himachal Pradesh, Kerala, Ladakh, Orissa, Rajasthan, Golden Temple, Taj Mahal, Wildlife.

Index

A

Adhinath 27, 36, 68
Adhinath Temple 69
adhishthana 43, 54, 69
airport (Khajuraho) 73, 109
Ajaygarh 20, 91
antarala 27
Archaeological Site Musuem 41, 74-75, 123
Archaeological Survey of India 21

B

Bandhavgarh Jungle Camp 95
Bandhavgarh Jungle Lodge 95
Bandhavgarh National Park 14, 95
Benisagar Lake 87
Bird Life 15-16
Brahma 24-25, 48, 50
Brahma Temple 18, 36, 63-65
Bundelkhandi 112
Bundella kingdom 90
Burt T.S. Capt. 21, 23, 54, 63

C

Canara Bank 121
Chandella dynasty 37
Chandella Hotel 89, 112
Chandella rulers 19-20, 44, 50, 54, 75, 87, 91, 94
Chattarpur 11, 21, 36-37
Chaturbhuj Temple 36, 63, 73
Chausat Yogini Temple 33, 36-37
Chattarpur state 88

Chitragupta Temple 25, 31, 50-51, 65
Circuit House 116
Climate 12, 108

D

Dantla hills 11, 53
Datia 80-82, 88
Devi Jagadambi Temple 25, 31, 41, 45, 48, 50-51, 65
Devi Mandap 40
Dharamshala 68, 116
Dhubela Museum 86
Dikpalas 26, 50, 68
Duladeo Temple 25, 31, 36, 72-73

E

Eastern Group of Temples 33, 62-65
erotic sculptures 30, 44, 54
Excursion Agents 126-127

F

Fauna 14-15
Festivals at Khajuraho 124-125
Flora 13-14

G

Ganesh 25, 44, 46, 54, 74-75
Ganga and Yamuna 27, 41, 86
Gangau Dam 87
garbha griha 27
Ghantai Temple 68
Gille's Tree House 89
Govind Mandir 81-82

H

Hanuman 62
Hari-Hara 73
Hinduism 24-25
History 18-21
Hospital 123
Hotel Chandella 112
Hotel Gautam 114
Hotel Jass Oberoi 114
Hotel Jhankar 115
Hotel Khajuraho Ashok 114
Hotel Payal 115
Hotel Rahil 116

I

Indian Airlines Office 109
inscriptions 19-20, 44, 54

J

Jahangir Mandir 83
Jain Group of Temples 68-71
Jain philosophy 27
Jain sculptures 74
Jain Temples 27, 36
Jarai Math temple 86
Javari Temple 36, 63, 73
Jhansi 80, 110
Jhansi Railway Station 110

K

Kalanjar 20, 94
Kandariya Mahadev Temple 25-26,
    31, 45-48, 50, 53, 69
Ken River 11, 88-89, 108
Ken River Lodge 89, 127
Khajur Sagar 15-16, 36, 62-63
Khuddar stream 36, 72
Krishna 45

L

Lakshman Temple 25, 31,
    40-45, 52-53
Lakshmi 68
Lal Bungalow 120
Lalguan Mahadev 18, 33
langur 15
Lavanya hills 73
Laxminarayan Temple 86
licensed guides 126
linga 25, 30, 38, 48, 54, 63,
    72, 94-95
Louis Rousselet 59

M

MP Tourism White
    Tiger Lodge 95
Madhya Pradesh 11-12, 14, 18
Madras Coffee Shop 119
Maha-Shivratri festival 31, 37,
    124
Mahadev Shrine 45, 48-50
mahamandap 27
Maharaja of Chattarpur 21, 36, 51
Mahavir 27
Mahoba 20, 87, 110
mahwa 13
mandap 27
mango 13
Matangeshvar Temple 25, 30-31,
    37-38

N

Nacchna 94-95
Nandi 25, 52-53
Nandi Mandap 52-53
Narasimha 45, 73
neem 13

New Punjab Open
  Air Restaurant 119
O
Orccha 82-86, 88
P
Pandav Falls 90
Panna 90-91
Panna Diamond Mines 91
Panna National Park 13-14,
  88-90, 127
Parshvanath 27, 31, 36, 69
Parshvanath Temple 68-69
Parvati 30-31, 44, 51, 69, 75
Parvati Temple 52
Photography 123
Pleasure Tours 127
Post and Telegraph Offices 121
pradakshina 26, 43

R
Rahilya 20
Rai Praveen Mahal 83
Raj Mahal 83
Raja Cafe 119
Rajgarh Palace 88, 127
Ram Raja Temple 83
Raneh Waterfalls 86-87, 127
Ranguan Lake 87
Religion 24-31
Restaurants 119-120

S
Sapta Matrikas 46
Satna 110
Shantinath 68
shikhara 26, 43, 45,
  48, 69, 72
Shilpa shastra 26

Shiv Sagar 15, 33, 36-37, 74
Shiva 24-25, 30-31, 36-38,
  44-46, 48, 50-54, 63, 69,
  72-75, 94-95
Shiv-ratri 37
Shopping 123
South-Eastern Group of Temples
  72-73
State Bank of India 121
Surya 51

T
teak 13, 90
Tirthankaras 27, 74
toran 48
Tour Aids 127
Tourist Bungalow 116
Tourist Information Counters 122
Tourist Village Complex 116

U
Umaria 95

V
Vamana 65
Vamana Temple 36, 65
Varaha 40-41, 45, 50, 53, 75
Varaha Mandap 40-41, 52
village of Khajuraho 36, 62,
  108, 112
Vindhyan range 11, 108
Vishnu 24-25, 40-41, 44-45
  48, 50, 63, 65, 68, 73, 74-75
Vishvanath Temple 25, 31, 45,
  52-55, 69

W
Western Group of Temples 33, 37,
  40-55, 74, 123